Anglesey and my Paint box by Pat Kaye

Dedicated to Harry Hamer our very close friend who also loved Anglesey, spending hundreds of hours waiting for fish on Llyn Alaw.

Published in the United Kingdom
by Patricia B. Kaye
Dorwyn
Four Mile Bridge
Holyhead
Anglesey
GWYNEDD.
LL65 2PJ

First printed by Cambrian Press
in August 2015.

2nd reprint 2020.

Cambrian Press Printers
Llanbadarn Road
Aberystwyth
SY23 3TN

Tel: +44(0)1970 613000
Fax +44(0)1970 615497

3rd reprint 2023.

Cambrian Press Printers

Layout —
Mel Parry
Benllech
melparree@btinternet.com

ISBN 978-0-9933562-0-9

Introduction.

Since 1968 two families drove from the other side of the Pennines in Yorkshire, through the Mountains of North Wales to spend three weeks of each year enjoying their Whitsun and Summer Holidays together on Holy Island, Anglesey.

The sun seemed to be generally blazing, the sea down at Rhoscolyn beach was always blue and we all had a great time together swimming, fishing, relaxing and getting on with all the other pastimes one enjoys on holiday.

A recent visit to the self same beach with one of the younger family members (now 45) with his young family and we are thrilled to see that little change has occured over the years in that particular location.

Eventually our families grew up and moved on, but even then we still visited on a regular basis, as the quietness and the beauty of the Island suited us. So much so that on retirement we decided to 'up sticks' and move to the area that we had come to enjoy.

It is now several years since we moved to Anglesey but we had not been living here long when an opportunity arose, for me to pursue my love of drawing — a recreation that I have enjoyed all of my life.

Presented with new sights, vistas and people, I felt the need to get out my pencil, pen and paint box and put into a Sketch book the things that I saw around me.

Ynys Môn is a lovely and varied Island, but most especially, for me, I saw that its people have made it the place that it has become.

Many people have visions and passions and are able to lead the way forwards by achieving their dreams.

In Anglesey the first real evidence of this is in the landscape and is possibly the "Ancient Standing Stones" that are dotted around the Island. Also the "Hut Circles" in which people lived their lives, and the "Burial Chambers" in which the old Islanders buried their dead. The time factor of the ancient constructions fill me with awe.

Small stone Churches spring up amongst the fields, both looking outwards towards the Sea, but also hidden in the Countryside. Fortunately most of these churches have been renovated over the long number of years by devout custodians and are in good repair, so that visitors are still able to enjoy their long History and Architecture.

There is evidence of the continual 'tussle' with the Sea that surrounds the Island. Brave men putting others needs before their own safety in cruel and often tumultous waters. The Lifeboats and Helicopters are our continual reminder.

The Tourist Industry which plays a huge part in the Commerce of the Island; and not to be forgotten the Farmers who cultivate the land.

All of these people make their mark by doing their own thing and quietly making up a 'Jigsaw' of the whole of the Island Community.

There are new Businesses (dreams) included in the Book and I hope that they are able to survive, but if not, then in the future others will follow and keep up with a Tenacity that the Islanders of Ynys Môn seem to be blessed with.

I hope that you enjoy my chosen sightings. I am aware that there are many that I have left out, for as I continually go around, my fingers itch to put down on paper other views, people and interesting buildings that I see. I apologise for the many that I have missed, but I sincerely hope that I have been able to capture what Ynys Môn means to me —
~ A fair Island with its big hearted Anglesey people.

You might even find new places to search out and visit after looking at the Book
~ Pat Kaye 2015

The Book starts with a Map of the Island.
I began at the Menai Bridge coming over on to the Island, and went down into Menai Town, from there on towards Beaumaris, and then continuing in an anti-clockwise direction around the Island, numbering places as I went. Eventually there are pages and places that don't fit in with the pattern, but they do have numbers and so should be simple to find on the map.

Enjoyment has been the order of the day for me as I have used the pen, pencil and paintbox. I hope you too find enjoyment from my choice of subjects.

Pat Kaye

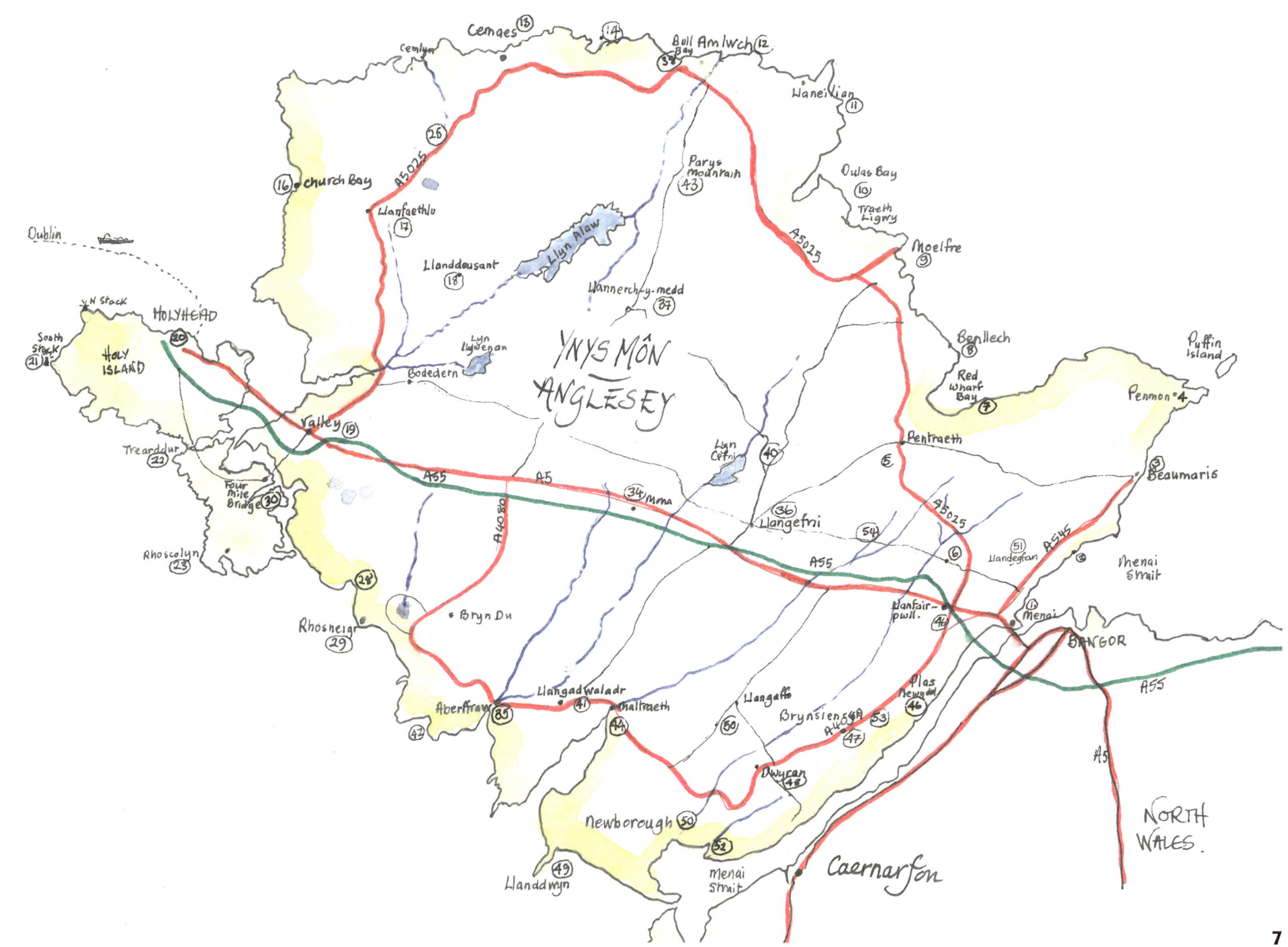

When one of my friends crosses the Bridge on to Anglesey she heaves a great sigh of relief — "home".

Menai Suspension Bridge.

What a spectacle for the Anglesey people to see this most marvellously elegant Bridge under construction. Mouths must have dropped open in awe. Designed by Thomas Telford a Scottish Engineer in 1818 and eventually opened in 1826. The cost was £120,000. Originally a toll was paid to cross the Bridge, and until 1941, the supporting chains were treated with linseed oil to prevent rust, but when the Bridge was strengthened in the 1930s, the chains were replaced by steel links. During 2005 the Bridge underwent its first complete repainting.

Just a stone's throw from the hugeness of the Bridge pillars is this sweet little white washed cottage by the side of the road. It is squeezed in and towered over by normal houses. Who lived here in the dim and distant past I wonder?

'The Liverpool' Arms, If walls could speak, no doubt there would be lots of colourful tales to hear.

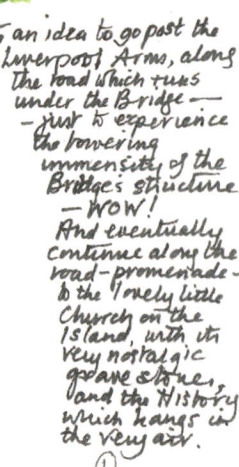

It's an idea to go past the Liverpool Arms, along the road which runs under the Bridge — just to experience the towering immensity of the Bridge's structure. — WOW! And eventually continue along the road-promenade — to the lonely little Church on the Island, with its very nostalgic gravestones, and the History which hangs in the very air.

①

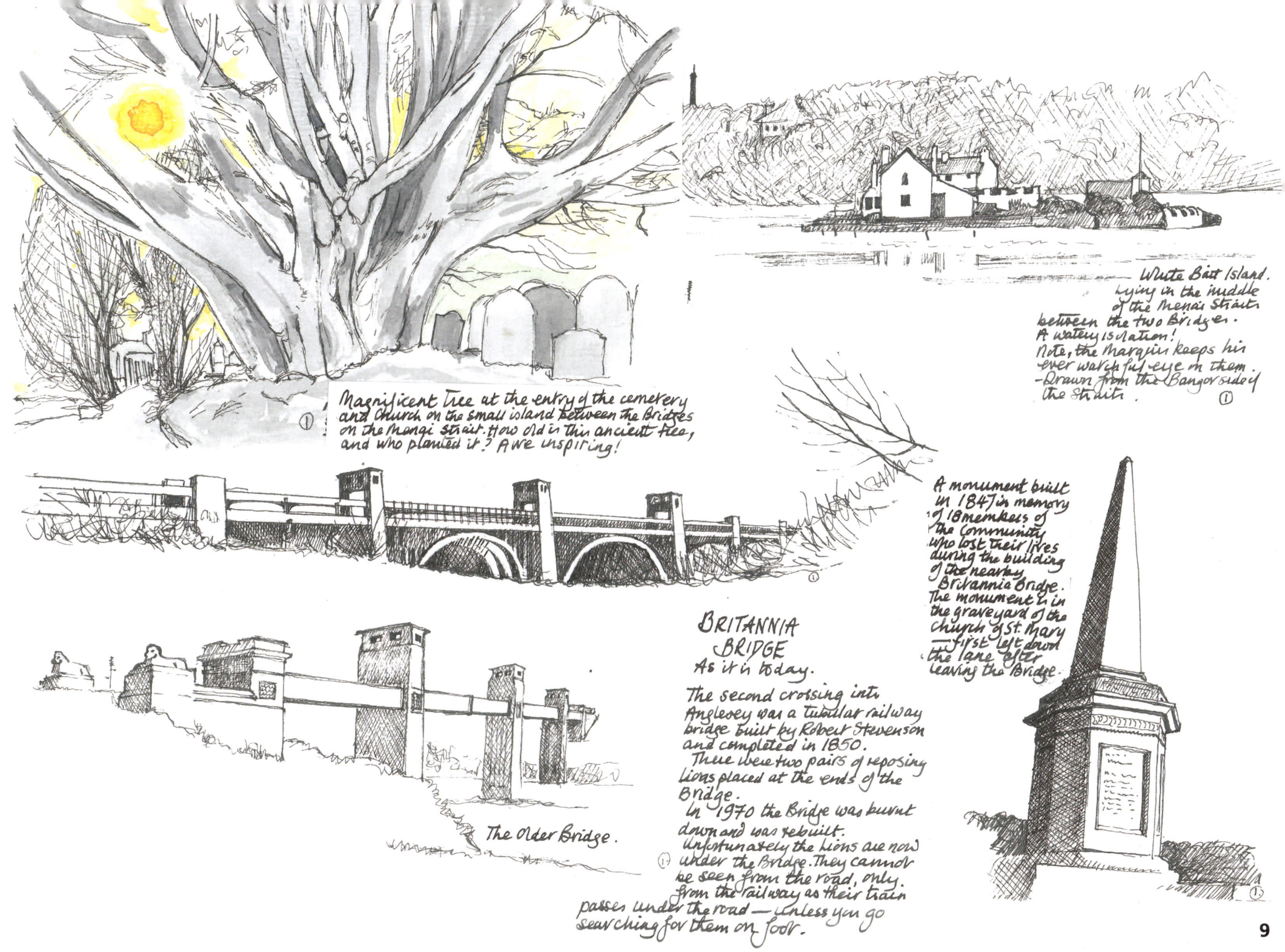

Magnificent Tree at the entry of the cemetery and church on the small island between the Bridges on the Menai Strait. How old is this ancient tree, and who planted it? Awe inspiring!

White Bait Island. Lying in the middle of the Menai Straits between the two Bridges. A watery isolation! Note, the Marquis keeps his ever watchful eye on them. —Drawn from the Bangor side of the Straits.

The Older Bridge.

BRITANNIA BRIDGE
As it is today.

The second crossing into Anglesey was a tubular railway bridge built by Robert Stevenson and completed in 1850.
There were two pairs of reposing Lions placed at the ends of the Bridge.
In 1970 the Bridge was burnt down and was rebuilt.
Unfortunately the Lions are now under the Bridge. They cannot be seen from the road, only from the railway as their train passes under the road — unless you go searching for them on foot.

A monument built in 1847 in memory of 18 members of the Community who lost their lives during the building of the nearby Britannia Bridge. The monument is in the graveyard of the church of St. Mary —first left down the lane after leaving the Bridge.

It's difficult to know what to say about this wonderful stone/yellow brick edifice which is down a side street in Menai. Clearly the flora and the tree on the roof love it and grow happily heavenwards. The front of the chapel now houses a fruit & vegetable market – a fine alternative to supermarket shopping. All must be very fresh

42a - Menai
A pleasing shop front selling interesting old and new artefacts! ①

A sign of the times. Chinese influence and an extravagant change to the Welsh grey! Situated in the back streets of Menai. ①

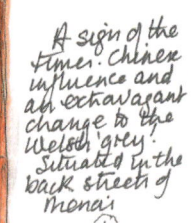

HORTUS MONENSIS

This small shop frontage is tucked away in a corner at Menai. It's easily overlooked but truly original. A gardening company work from here. ①

① Who built this old mariner? Who sailed & fished in her and when? Gradually rotting into the mud – SAD! A plant via a bird has found its way here too!

Boat building yard "Mooring & storage Repairs." What a surprise on the side of the Straits behind Menai.

The comparisons are marvellous old boats & fabulous yachts
① New marinas and fantastic tin sheds. – A place for everyone and everything

Early Tourism in Anglesey 6

This old photograph which is reproduced in the 'Anglesey Guide' quite fascinates me, and to use a pen to copy all these wonderful Edwardians is a real joy for me. It becomes obvious that the passengers on the Paddle Steamer — 'La Marguerite' are very well heeled. White collars, ties, bowlers & caps for the trip are obviously necessary — and the ladies hats are fabulous.

The Marguerite was a paddle steamer transferred from the Thames Estuary by the Liverpool and North Wales Steamship Company and operated from Liverpool to the Piers of Bangor and Beaumaris. No doubt many of these people were bound for the Bulkeley Hotel or other holiday venues. (L)

The Paddle Steamer —
'LA MARGUERITE'
The boat is thronged with the
Edwardians all in their finery.

Menai.
Two young men who are determined to make their mark in Anglesey.

Glyn Davies captures the essence of Anglesey in every dramatic photograph with the aid of his camera. The seas are magnificent, the atmosphere in the weather is compelling; the sun rising; the moon waning; the rain and the wind are all captured with his certain eye.

His photographs are compiled in his handsome books and it's also possible to purchase large signed framed photographs at his small Gallery down the hill below the Church.

Benjamin Lee has his Chocolate and Cake making business across the road and around the corner from Glyn. If you enjoy chocolate, as you enter his shop you enter paradise, as the aroma of chocolate is overwhelming. To look around and see his gravity defying inventive cakes is a joy. We loved the cake with all the Wedding Group sitting around the "Top Table". The thought of eating the mother-in-law is very amusing. We also enjoyed seeing a huge cake covered in stilettoes. Benjamin certainly has a sense of humour.

Two young men who are to be commended in their determination to encourage the visitors over the Bridge to the Island.

Glyn Davies

A Valentine window ①

① ①

Dylan's Restaurant - Menai Bridge.
The jolly vehicle sits outside reminding
customers of the Restaurant just down the lane.
On a wet day we found the Restaurant fully
booked, but we were allowed to sit outside on
the balcony with welsh blanket on our seats and
on our laps and the heating switched on above
us. We sat enjoying our meal and the open views
across the Straits.
Great to be so cheerfully looked after.
The Restaurant & Chocolate shop are
comparatively new to Menai and are a
real asset to both Menai and the bigger
picture of Anglesey.   (1.)

11

13

Hawthorn Yard — Menai
Situated on the main street to the right.
'Jane' in her own little kingdom selling small and large pieces of her chosen furniture and collectables.
Tourists as well as Anglesey people make a bee line for her shop. Buy whatever takes your fancy to beautify your home.
①

St. Mary's Church at Menai
A grand affair with a spire ready to 'blast off' like a rocket!

①

A handsome chapel up a side road further along the main street.

Towards the end of the village on the right is a lovely Gallery — ORIEL TEGFRYN. Regular Exhibitions are held here and its a good place to go if you wish to fill a space on one of your walls and enjoy looking at
① ART.

Struggling to get likenesses, but who could resist this careful chap against the beautiful stained glass corridor in Plas Rhianfa. We learned that this careful chap had once owned this magnificent building and now worked for the Hotel Chain. After a very varied career he seems happy keeping everything intact at Rhianfa. ②

Plas Rhianfa and a few eye catching items.

And a chinese pot.

Up and down to let down those golden locks. The spiral staircase in between buildings.

Delft tiles set into a wall in a row.

A pair of handsome bookcases, one in each corner of a lounge.

A pair of tall parrots.

Down some steps in this narrow room is this a font?

Look upwards to see a fine light fitting and two splendid ceilings - one painted plaster and one beautifully beamed.

A pair of finely framed bird studies down a corridor.

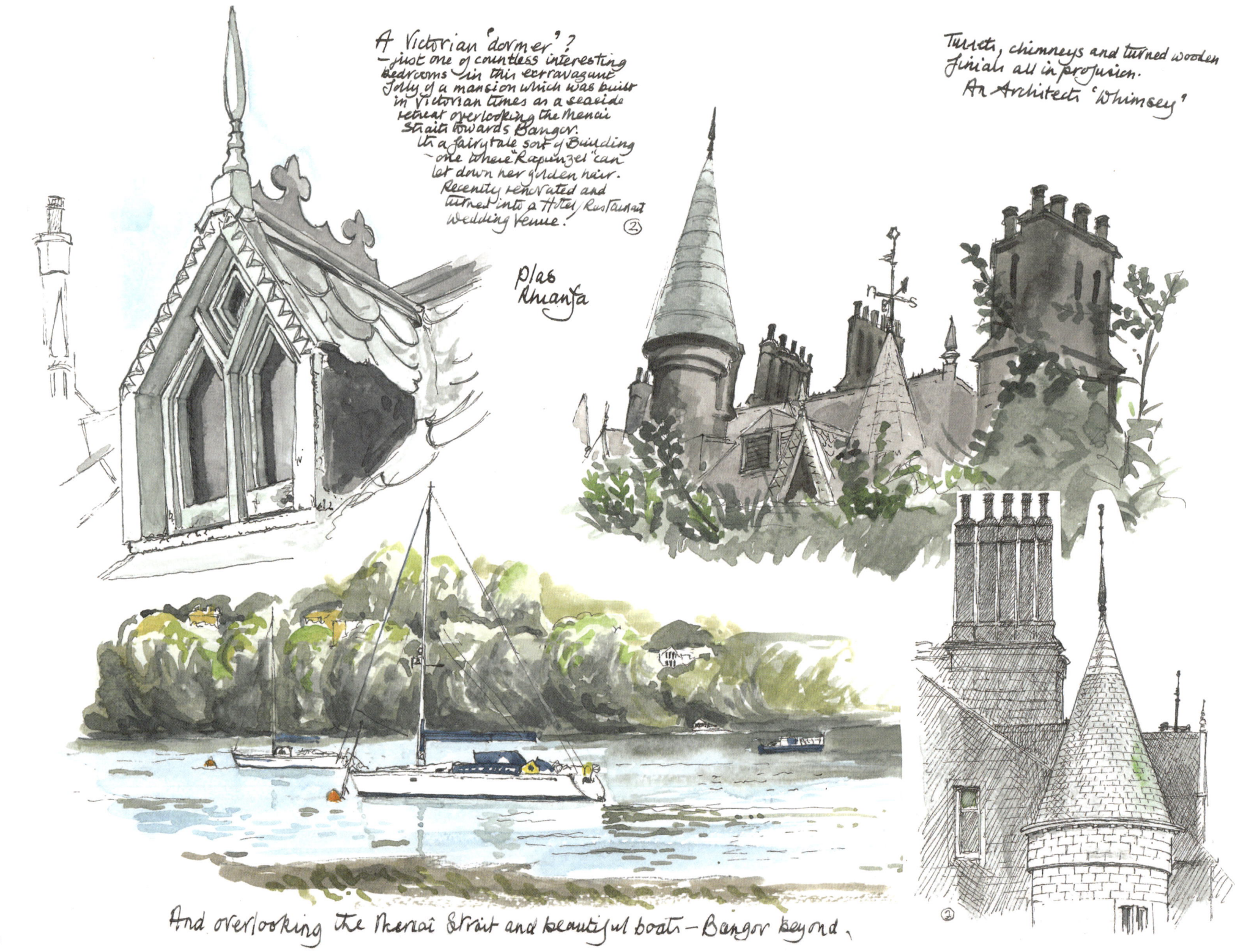

A Victorian "dormer"?
— just one of countless interesting
bedrooms in this extravagant
folly of a mansion which was built
in Victorian times as a seaside
retreat overlooking the Menai
Straits towards Bangor.
It's a fairytale sort of Building
— one where "Rapunzel" can
let down her golden hair.
Recently renovated and
turned into a Hotel/Restaurant
Wedding Venue.   ②

Plas
Rhianfa

Turrets, chimneys and turned wooden
finials all in profusion.
An Architect's "Whimsey"

And overlooking the Menai Strait and beautiful boats — Bangor beyond.

Plas Rhianfa.
Built in 1849-51 for
Sir John Hay Williams whose
main residence was Bodelwyddan on the
mainland. Its fine slate roofs and turrets
give it the appearance of a small French
chateau.
It has recently been purchased and renovated by an Hotel Company. Visitors are welcome
to its complex interior and Wedding Parties seem
to be the order of the day. Now known as
Chateau Rhianfa. ②

They do say - "from
the sublime to the
rediculous." Choose which
you will. All are wonderful
examples of the Architect
Builders artistry. The little
black and white house purports
to be built around 1400 and
to be one of the oldest in
Gt. Britain.
The main street in Beaum-
aris can be described as
being similar to a film set.
I love its quirkyness:
It improves all the time.

Around the corner
behind the Main street is
a very colourful shopping
experience. Beautiful furnishing
fabrics can be purchased and also whacky gifts,
The plants are incredible in Summer in this
sunny sheltered square and there is quite a
Mediterranean Air.

③

③

17

Times Past — 1907

Drawing done from a photograph found in 'Edwardian
Anglesey II' by John Covell.
    Edward VII and the Royal Party being entertained for tea on
the terrace of another imposing mansion — Baron Hill in 1907.
(It overlooked Beaumaris but now sadly is in ruins).
    The King had come to North Wales to lay the foundation stone at
Bangor University College.
    Seated from the left — Sir Richard Bulkeley, Queen Alexandra,
Lady Magdalen Bulkeley, Edward VII, Miss Siriol Bulkeley,
Princess Victoria and the Countess Gosforth.
    Standing — H.R. of Kinmel and Lord Tweedsmouth.

    Imagine carrying this concoction on one's head
                while having a cup of tea and a cake.
                        Perfect balance?

courtesy
of John
Covell.
(Edwardian)
Anglesey

18

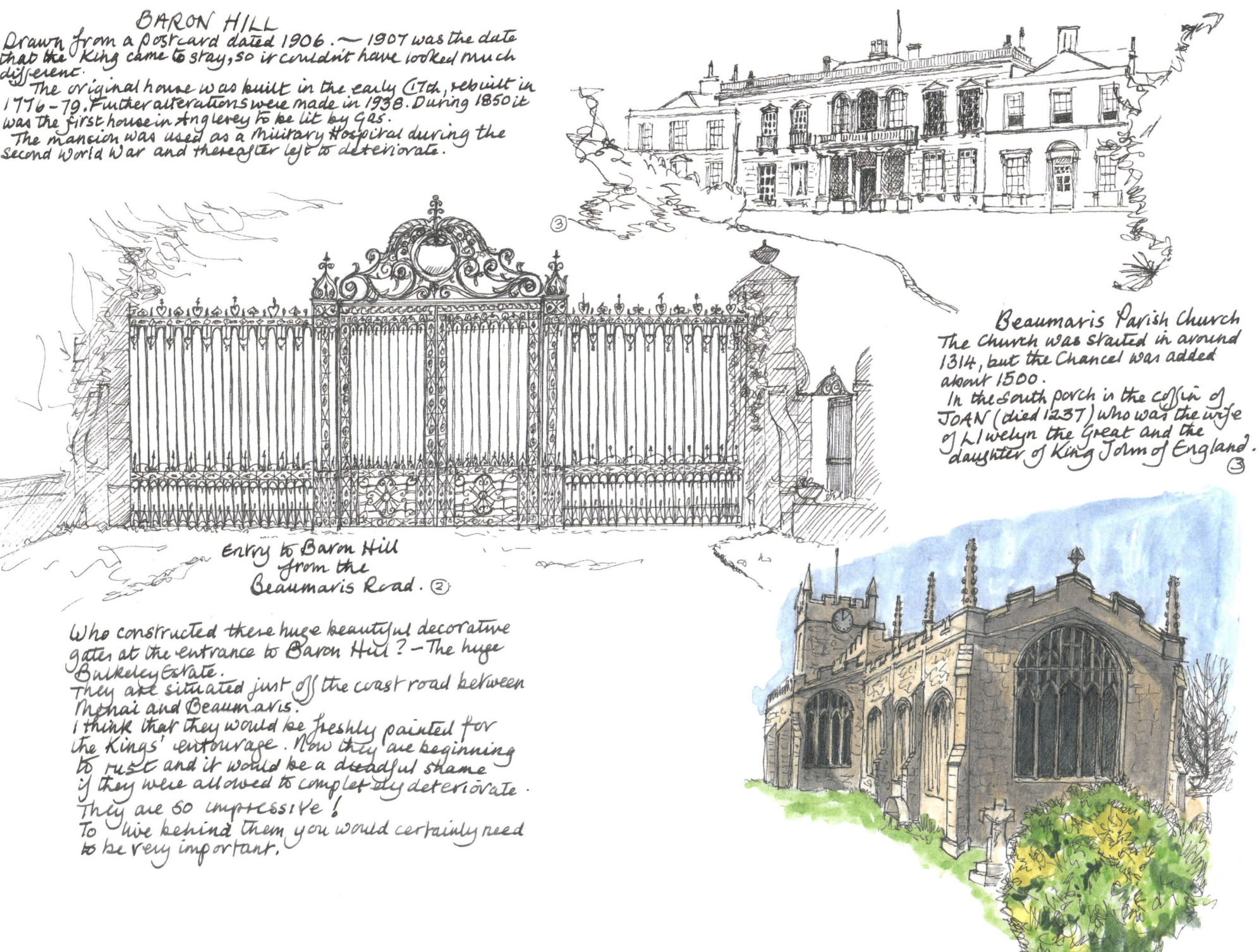

BARON HILL

Drawn from a postcard dated 1906. — 1907 was the date that the King came to stay, so it couldn't have looked much different.

The original house was built in the early C17th, rebuilt in 1776-79. Further alterations were made in 1938. During 1850 it was the first house in Anglesey to be lit by Gas.

The mansion was used as a Military Hospital during the second world War and thereafter left to deteriorate.

③

Entry to Baron Hill
from the
Beaumaris Road. ②

Who constructed these huge beautiful decorative gates at the entrance to Baron Hill? — The huge Bulkeley Estate.
They are situated just off the coast road between Menai and Beaumaris.
I think that they would be freshly painted for the Kings' entourage. Now they are beginning to rust and it would be a dreadful shame if they were allowed to completely deteriorate.
They are so impressive!
To live behind them you would certainly need to be very important.

Beaumaris Parish Church
The Church was started in around 1314, but the Chancel was added about 1500.
In the south porch is the coffin of JOAN (died 1237) who was the wife of Llwelyn the Great and the daughter of King John of England.
③

A handsome 'Wedgewood' schoolroom ③

And a lemon Yellow chapel ③

The old Court House '1614' ③

Chique Kids .Childrens

MOUNT-PLEASANT

ROSE HILL

LITTLE LANE

GWYNDY GOAL ST.

ROSEMARY LANE

MARGARET STREET

RATING ROW

Every which way you turn in Beaumaris each busy home or shop owner has been active with a tin of coloured paint. All Architectural features are picked out, so that the whole effect is a Paint Box of delectable colour.
To walk around the streets on a sunny Summer day is quite a delight.
Reading in "Ward-Lock's" North Wales (date unknown - 30's?) it states — "Except for the Church and the Castle it has few buildings of Architectural merit but the place has an 'air' that is very attractive to those from bustling and smoke shrouded cities."
As you must imagine I find the Author quite wrong about the Architecture

③

The lodge and entrance to the Castle.

Originally the moat was connected to the sea and gave protection to boats.

Beaumaris Castle.
The Castle was the eighth built by Edward I with which he intended to 'crush' the Welsh. It was built between 1295 and 1298. Walls within walls and the whole surrounded by a moat.

A well cared for Chapel. But now well cared for Apartment. It would be interesting to enter and see the transformations.

A Sign outside the "OLD BULLS HEAD" - a posting inn founded in the 1470's - rebuilt in the 17th. Shakespeare is reputed to have stayed here. A good meal is to be had in the Restaurant or lunch in the Bistro downstairs.

③

Oriel Janet Bell Gallery

Janet Bell featured on BBC Countryfile painting bluebells

Examples of
Janets own work.

"IT IS NOT AN ARTISTS
JOB TO PLEASE
ANYONE
BUT TO BRAVELY
DO THE WORK THAT
THEY ARE MOST
COMPELLED TO DO
ITS THE PUBLICS JOB
TO BRAVELY
SEEK OUT AND
APPRECIATE THE WORK
THAT RESONATES
WITH THEM "

(seen on her web)
page !

The Janet Bell Gallery.

Janet is a young lady who has 'bravely'
built up her Gallery Business over the
last few years. Initially she had a smaller
space in a back street, but was able eventually
to move on to the main street of Beaumaris.
Besides selling her own work (originals,
prints and cards etc.) she branched out
selling the work of other Artists and Craft
workers.
The Gallery is well worth a visit, as there
is generally some new piece of work to see
and hopefully to take home with you.
On holiday its a good idea to buy BRITISH. ③

Beau's Tea Room – Beaumaris.

Valentine Week.
charming window from which you might purchase an old cup and saucers; a tea set or a 'knitted' bun or piece of cake. Better still, purchase a real cake or piece of Barabrith and eat it with a good cup of tea. ③

Next to the oldest house on the High Street is this lovely old fashioned tea-room, painted with a pretty "Icing pink" colour. ③
Beau's Tea Rooms

Individuality in Beaumaris.

23

③
Just a corner of the Castle at Beaumaris. The monumental Victorian water pumps are structures in the library grounds dated 1867.

③
Former Grammar School. The beautifully proportioned old building is connected to Beaumaris's Library. It provides a lovely space for Exhibitions. The stone above the door is dated 1603.

Another important seagull sitting atop a strategic point near to Penmon

DANGER
NO PASSAGE
BETWEEN LIGHTHOUSE
AND LAND

Penmon lighthouse on a quiet day. Warning of 'No Passage Landwards' So Sailor BEWARE!
④

④
Man's mark yet again - more simply done in a lighthearted way. How long will these two feet tell the viewer that 'HE' had been here and given the date when a concrete job was done in 2007.

Coastguards homes overlooking the handsome lighthouse - A bleak enough place when the winds are howling and the sea is raging in wintertime. Lovely in the sun!
④

24

One of the Ticket kiosks at Beaumaris. "Roll up, roll up and get your tickets here for a fishing trip or to see the Puffins at Puffin Island. ③

Penmon Priory and Dovecote.

SAILOR'S RETURN Est 1800

Free House
Restaurant
Accommodation

Beaumaris
~ Another Pub.
with a long past.
~ no doubt
interesting and
colourful tales to
tell if the walls
could speak - or
to keep quiet about!
③

A puffin
inhabitant of
Puffin Island
near to Penmon.

Apologies to
Tunnicliffe - the most
wonderful and renowned
Artist for his pictures,
sketches and illustrations
of birds and wildlife. See lots of
examples at Oriel Ynys môn · Llangefni.

Tradition dates the foundation of the Priory to the
reign of Maelgwn Gwynedd who died in AD 547.
The original Church was probably destroyed by Vikings in 971.
The replacement was built between 1120 and 1170.
The monks were disciplined in the 13th century by the Romans.
The Monastery was dissolved about 1537 and passed to the Bulkeley Estates.
The 13th century chancel was partly rebuilt in 1855 - a trim Victorian place of
worship is still used for services.
Penmon dovecote probably was erected by Sir Richard Bulkeley
of Baron Hill about 1600. Inside the building is a stone pillar
which once supported ladders to almost 1000 pigeon holes. The birds
provided eggs and meat - no doubt to the Priory
④

STONE SCIENCE at Llanddyfnan, near Pentraeth
It is a hugely informative venture, run by an owner who is truly devoted to his subject. There are thousands of exhibits, many of which are thousands and even millions of years old. They are often displayed against interesting back drops.
It's possible to purchase a little piece of History to take away from the well stocked shop.
The building is built aptly into the side of an old lime quarry. A wonderful visit for an inquisitive child — or an adult. ⑤

A Reconstructed MAMMOTH — Wow!

STONE SCIENCE

STONE SCIENCE

Ancient 'fossils' — from rocks.

Imparting information — you only have to ask and the answers are given.

PILI
PALAS ⑥
Nature world
Menai Bridge
Experience a sub-
tropical world with
lush foliage where
exotic butterflies
flutter and feed, —
and even land upon you
if you are lucky.
   There are also birds,
lizards, snakes and
terrapins; even a
farm yard, a play
area for children,
a café and a shop.
— lots of fun for the
    afternoon!

27

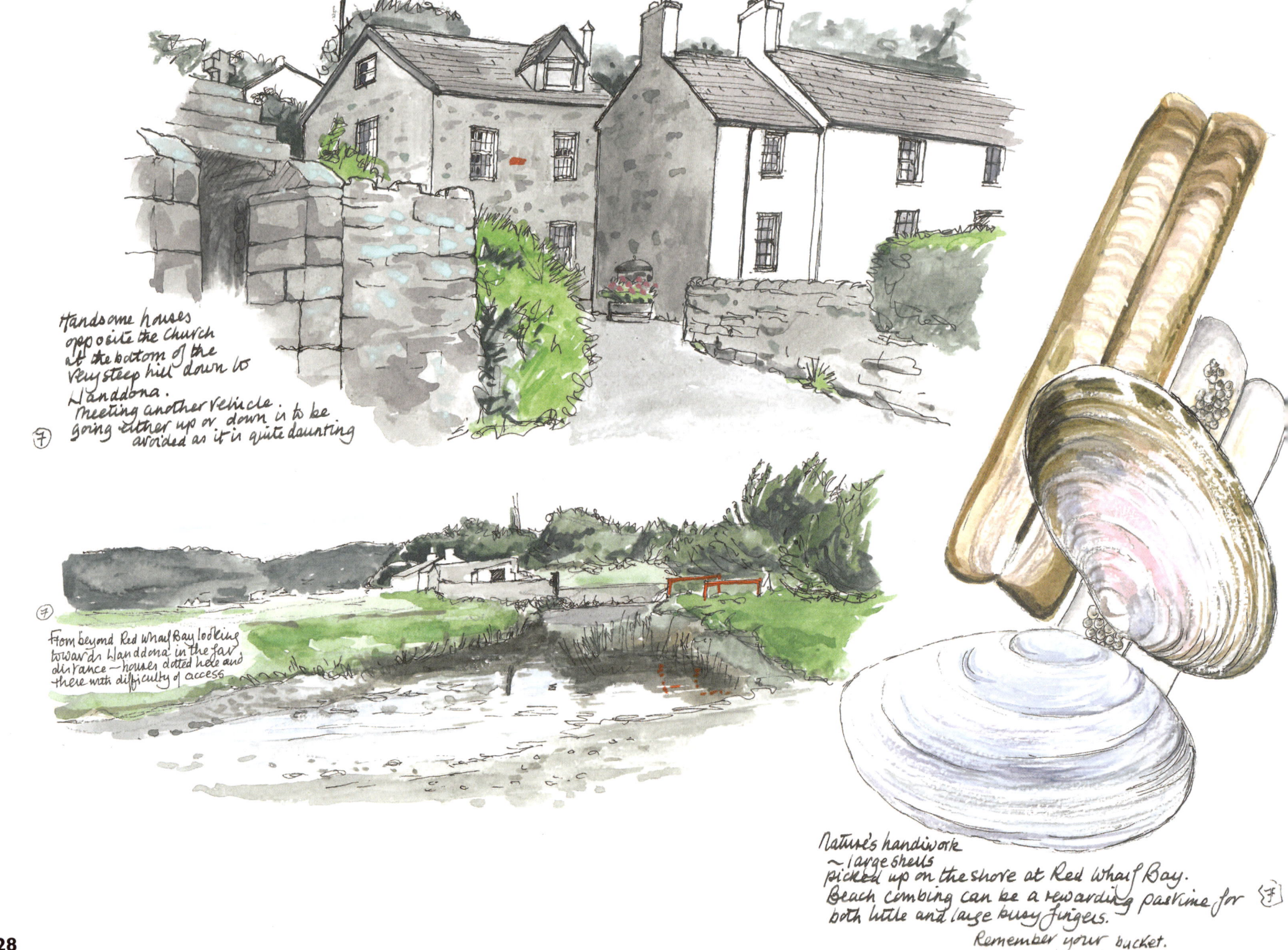

Handsome houses
opposite the Church
at the bottom of the
very steep hill down to
Llanddona.
Meeting another vehicle
going either up or down is to be
avoided as it is quite daunting

From beyond Red Wharf Bay looking
towards Llanddona in the far
distance — houses dotted here and
there with difficulty of access

Nature's handiwork
~ large shells
picked up on the shore at Red Wharf Bay.
Beach combing can be a rewarding pastime for
both little and large busy fingers.
Remember your bucket.

28

Red Wharf Bay & Benllech.
Listening to a programme on T.V.,
I hear that the University of Bangor
are doing research into ancient
clams which thrive on the sands,
particularly at Red Wharf Bay.
A lovely place to rummage about on
the sands and then go in or sit outside
for a tasty lunch.

The Ship Inn on the coast
at Red Wharf Bay.
At the bottom of a steep hill
on the right.
A grand place to eat your
lunch and particularly on
a chilly day in front of a
roaring fire. ⑦

SHIP INN
FREE HOUSE

Headland
properties at
Benllech.
It is a very popular holiday
resort as the sands are so
good for children.

EVENING MEAL

MOELFRE LIFEBOAT
16
14
12

The Seafarer's Hymn
— William Whiting
Eternal Father, strong to save
whose arm doth bind the restless wave,
who bidd'st the mighty ocean deep
its own appointed limits keep:
O hear us when we cry to thee
For those in peril on the sea.
AND Hear us, O Lord, from Heaven, thy dwelling place,
Like them of old, in vain we toil all night.
Unless with us thou go, who art the light,
Come then, O Lord, that we might see thy face

Thou Lord dost rule the raging of the sea
When loud the storm and furious is the gale
Strong is thine arm; our little
barques are frail
Send us thy help;
remember Galilee.
"W.H.Gui" — PEEL CASTLE.

And how often
has this hefty
old Anchor
seen its days
in fathoms
deep?
The Anchor is
fixed to the wall
going down to
the beach and
opposite Anne's
Pantry.
⑨

What a lovely surprise
to see a great swathe of
these showy flowers cling-
-ing to the rocks on the
cliffs. They are a brilliant
psych-edelic pink whilst the
fleshy leaves are strangely triangular
in section. They are part of the
mesembryanthemum family – our garden
variety paled into comparison to this fantastic
extended and natural show.

Two fine Sculptures
to be seen on a headland
garden near to the Lifeboat
station at Moelfre –
–Two past shipwrecks.

Moelfre

The Kinmel Arms
Moelfre

overlooking
the Bay

Up at the top of the hill above
the bay, this charming little Wood
Shop is a surprise. Also a large
supply of second hand books.
Reading matter for your
HOLS!

An interesting café/shop window in
Moelfre. Possible to eat in the shop or in
the garden or forecourt outside – hopefully
in the sunshine
~ Ann's Pantry.

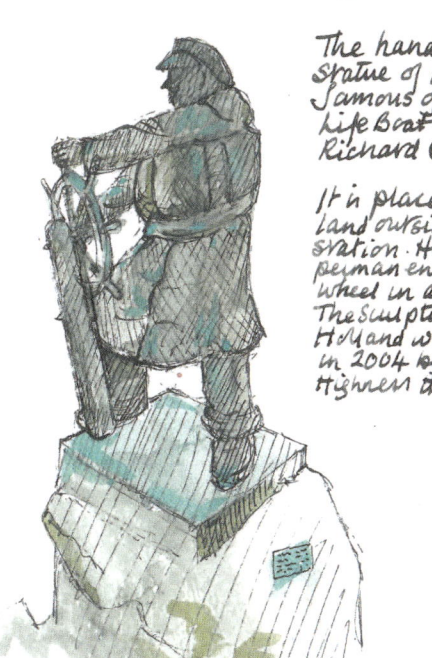

The handsome Bronze
statue of the most
famous of Moelfre's
Life Boat men –
Richard Evans (1905 –
2001).
It is placed on the Head-
land outside the lifeboat
station. He is now
permanently at his
wheel in all weathers.
The sculpture by Sam
Holland was unveiled
in 2004 by His Royal
Highness the Prince of Wales.

Boats pulled up on the shingle
in front of handsome cottages
overlooking the Bay. Climb the
hill and turn the corner and
on the left is a very well
equipped gift shop and café.
The area seems quite different to the rest of
Anglesey. The pretty village is quite hilly,
the beach is shingly pebbles and the sea
around these coasts have endangered
many lives with countless shipwrecks.
We really enjoyed our couple of
hours spent in this 'olde worldly' place
from our enjoyment of the 'cuppa' and
the Bara brith in Ann's Pantry to the
choosing of a few paperbacks in the Wood
shop, and to feeling the wind on our faces
as we admired the handsome sculpture.
There is also a very pleasant headland walk.

Bring me
sunshine
In your smile
☺

We all need
more
happiness

Bring me
laughter
all the while

Bring me fun
Bring me
sunshine

In this World
that we
live ♪

Bring me
love ♥

Llugwy Beach — Vast stretches of open sands,
sea and sky. A perfect holiday beach for digging, running, swimming
and just enjoying with the family of children.
The small jolly café with its touch of humour must be an added bonus if you
don't want to take your own 'sarnies' for the day and probably a meeting place for the young!
Only open in the Summer months.

⑩ Dulas Beach — higher up the coast
— wrecked boat — more stories to be
read into this!

32

The Church of
Saint Eilian.

The Oak Screen carved in
the 15th by a long forgotten
craftsman with the 18th.
painting of a skeleton in
the centre
SCARY!

Saint Eilian.
Timeless beauty in
the North Western
corner of Anglesey.

could you
squeeze into the
ancient oak chest
which had been used to collect
offerings from medieval pilgrims?

A craftsmans lovely
settle.

The sting of death is sin!

A window in Saint Eilian's
chapel 'tucked in'
behind the church.
And the old Shrine.

33

From the Anglesey Guide — Philip Steele & Robert Williams:

The Tower of St. Eilian's Church dates from the ⑫th, but the nave and chancel were built between 1480-81, as indicated by dated stones on the exterior of the Church.
Dating of the roof is around 1480 too.
An unusual pyramidal spire surmounts a broad tower.
Sensitive repairs were undertaken in 1929 and also in 2002.

The corner structure on the South side was added in 1614 as a passageway to St. Eilian's Chapel.
The Chapel is thought to overlie the grave of the Saint.
A marked difference in the alignments of Chapel and Church, suggests that the Chapel predates the ⑫th Church.
The late ⑮th rood screen features the ⑰th or ⑱th painting of the skeleton.
The chest is 250 years old and at Llaneilian in order to ensure a long life, the custom was to try and lie in the Oak Chest. Who hammered all those nails into the ancient chest? And how many souls clambered into the chest expecting to add years to their age. We all wish it were so easy.
The Church is noted for its wooden carvings, so search diligently and you might spot angels playing flutes and the double fishes seen below, along with other interesting artefacts.

I personally am intrigued with the yin-yang fish — dark/light negative/positive male/female
The concept of duality forming a whole.
— an ancient Chinese concept, but occasionally used by myself in a fish plate design.

Point Lymas Lighthouse.

Built in 1853 for £1,165 by the trustees of Liverpool Docks, although there had been a lighthouse on the North Coast since 1766.
Originally it was a simple operation using two oil lamps and reflectors — from a farm house — not far away from this existing building.

Sailing by, minding its own business!

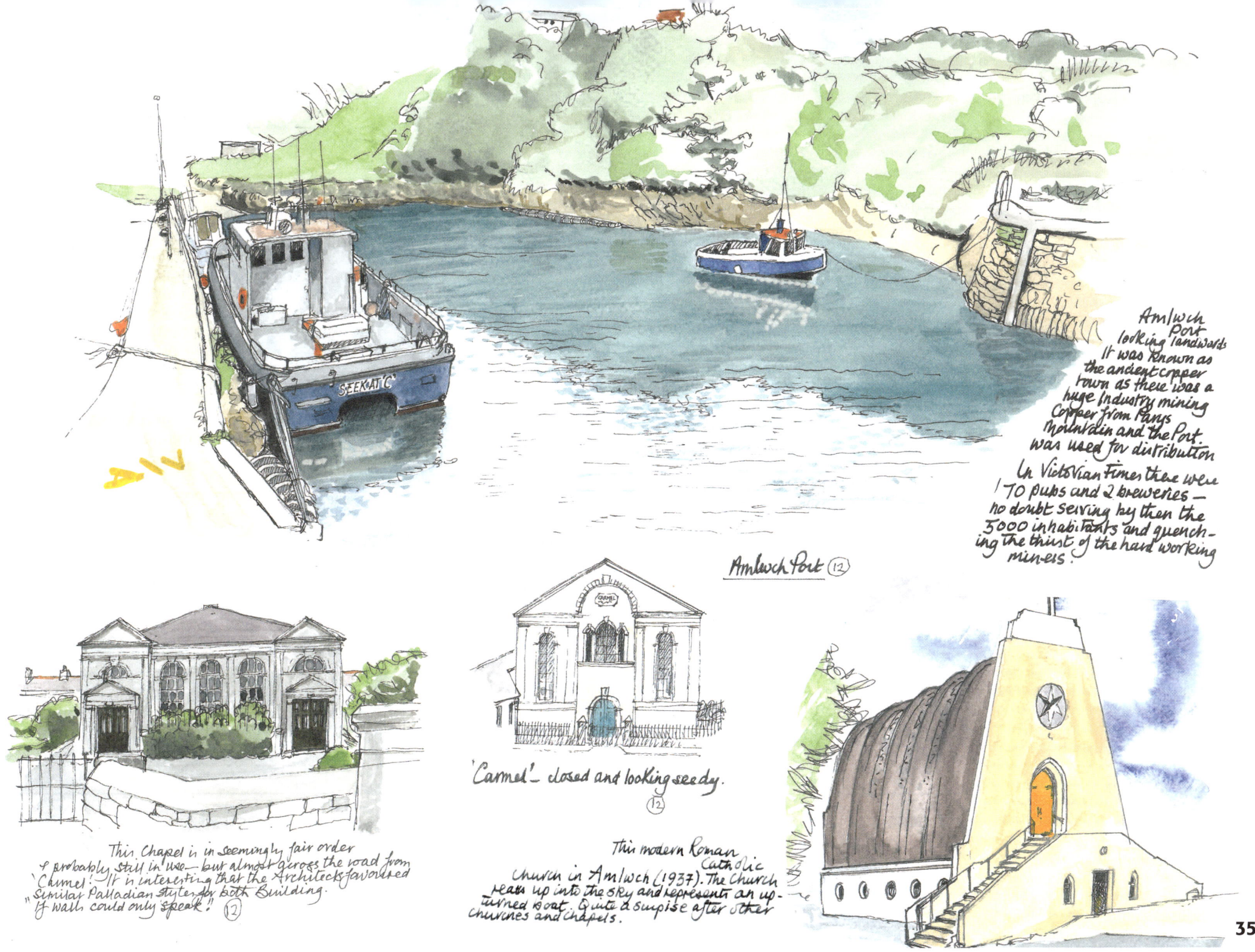

Amlwch Port looking landwards. It was known as the ancient copper town as there was a huge industry mining copper from Parys Mountain and the Port was used for distribution.

In Victorian times there were 170 pubs and 2 breweries — no doubt serving by then the 5000 inhabitants and quenching the thirst of the hard working miners.

Amlwch Port ⑫

'Carmel' — closed and looking seedy. ⑫

This Chapel is in seemingly fair order & probably still in use — but almost across the road from 'Carmel'. It is interesting that the Architects favoured similar Palladian styles for both Building. "If walls could only speak!" ⑫

This modern Roman Catholic Church in Amlwch (1937). The Church rears up into the sky and represent an upturned boat. Quite a surprise after other churches and chapels.

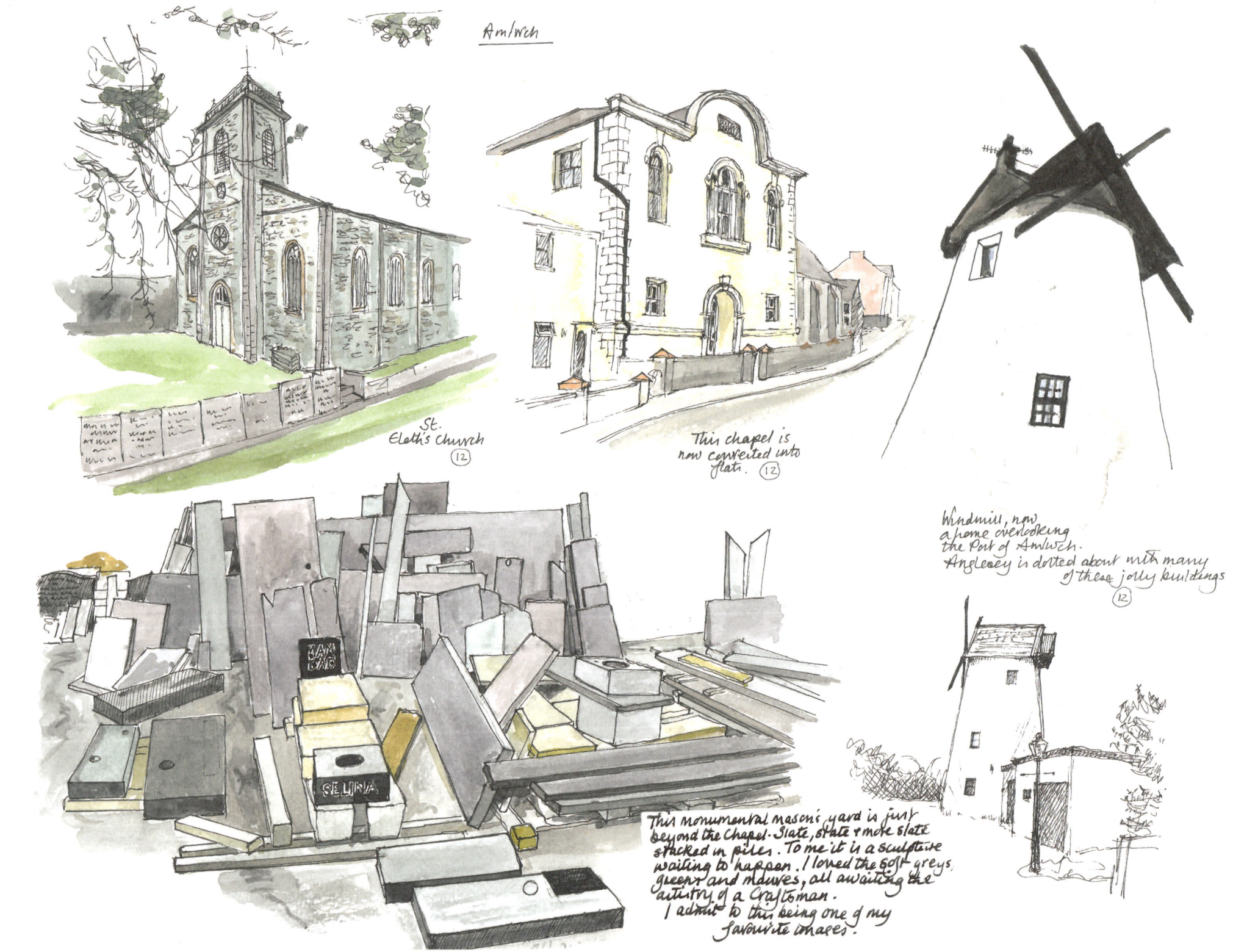

Amlwch

St. Eleth's Church (12)

This chapel is now converted into flats. (12)

Windmill, now a home overlooking the Port of Amlwch. Anglesey is dotted about with many of these jolly buildings (12)

This monumental mason's yard is just beyond the Chapel. Slate, slate & more slate stacked in piles. To me it is a sculpture waiting to happen. I loved the soft greys, greens and mauves, all awaiting the artistry of a Craftsman.
I admit to this being one of my favourite images.

MAM DAD

SELINA

The Copper Mine head
from the road going over
Parys Mountain.

(12) The Heritage Centre
at Amlwch Port has a
small Exhibition about
Parys Mountain, the
rock and descriptions
of the miners work etc.

Copper Kingdom. (43)

A great copper chasm is the result of a mountain of
coppery rock being dismantled by hand and being
sent worldwide from the little port of Amlwch.

The boom began in 1778 although metal had been
extracted 4000 years ago. The mines finally closed
in 1880, but it had employed a workforce of 1200, men
women and children. Wages were fourpence a day
but the owner - Thomas Williams (1737-1802) was known
locally as Twm Chwarae Teg (Tom fair play). The work was
obviously dangerous and hard. Initially it was carried out
in deep opencast pits, but later shafts were sunk.

Parys mountain's copper mineral is in the form of
Chalcopyrite - $CuFeS_2$. This is often concentrated in veins
through Quartz. Women workers hammered the quartz
into small pieces to extract the ore ready for smelting.
They were known as the Capa ladies.

The hollowed out resultant space glows in reds,
browns, purple, ochre and orange. It is a huge
spectacle and the thoughts of all those people spending
their working lives toiling in this great pit feels
quite shocking. — Its what people did for
their survival, and to keep
their families.

Anglesey Pennies

The pennies and half pennies were
produced between 1787-93 when copper
coinage was in short supply.

Apparently 10 million were minted
they are so beautifully designed, that
I wonder about the Craftsman. The
lettering on the back is quite lovely.

Cemaes Bay ⑬

'Ye olde Vigour' — a few strides away from 'The Stag'! ⑬

A tangle of chain on the beach.

A decorative border of red brick and a small panel enhancing a very plain row of small terrace houses in Cemaes Bay ⑬

Well cared for colourful homes on the Main Street in Cemaes Bay ⑬

How nice to have this very happy sounding name next to your front door.

JOLLY SAILOR

The 'Stag' at the bottom of the Main Street and above the Harbour at Cemaes Bay

Everything is especially tidy in this seaside village.

Cemaes Bay

Two Chapels either side
of Cemaes Bay Main Street —
— just yards apart. There must
have been a very interesting
history here — and competition
— well?
I am consistently inquisitive
to learn about the persons
who made decisions on colour
schemes.
Each Chapel must have
its TOWER.

A few boats
at Cemaes Bay
⑬

Handsome healthy looking cows munching happily at Wylfa. ⑬

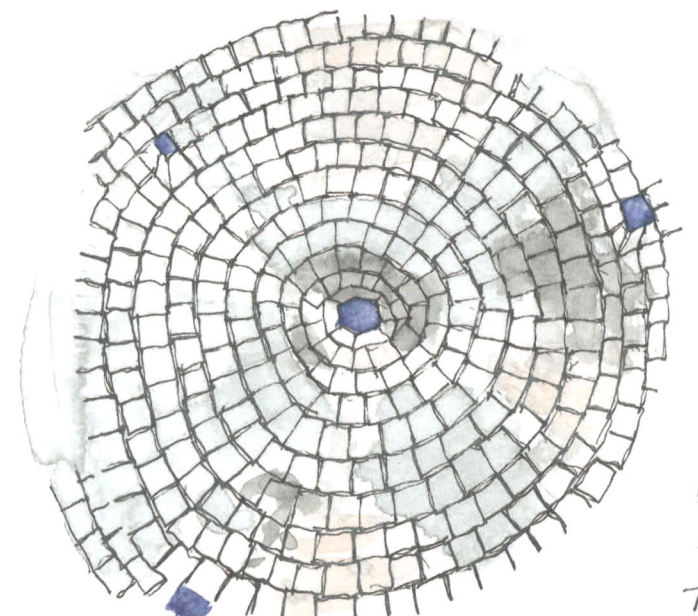

concentric decorative rings of bricks forming the roof of one of the Beehive shaped Kilns ~ beware if you enter.

The ruined Porth Wen Brickworks which operated between 1889 and 1924 and which was finally abandoned in the 1930's. Bricks were produced for building using Quartzite from the nearby cliffs. The Kilns and paths are quite delapidated and dangerous, so care must be taken. Who decided in 1889 that bricks should be produced here, using the material that the cliffs had to offer ~ intriguing!
⑭

An entrance to one of the 'Beehives'. Beware! please note crumbling structures, but what lovely Buildings, crying out to be preserved.
⑭

Having been a Potter all my life I found the Kilns exciting. It must have been quite thrilling to see them glowing red and full of BRICKS.

An interior of a Kiln with space for lots of BRICKS! ⑭

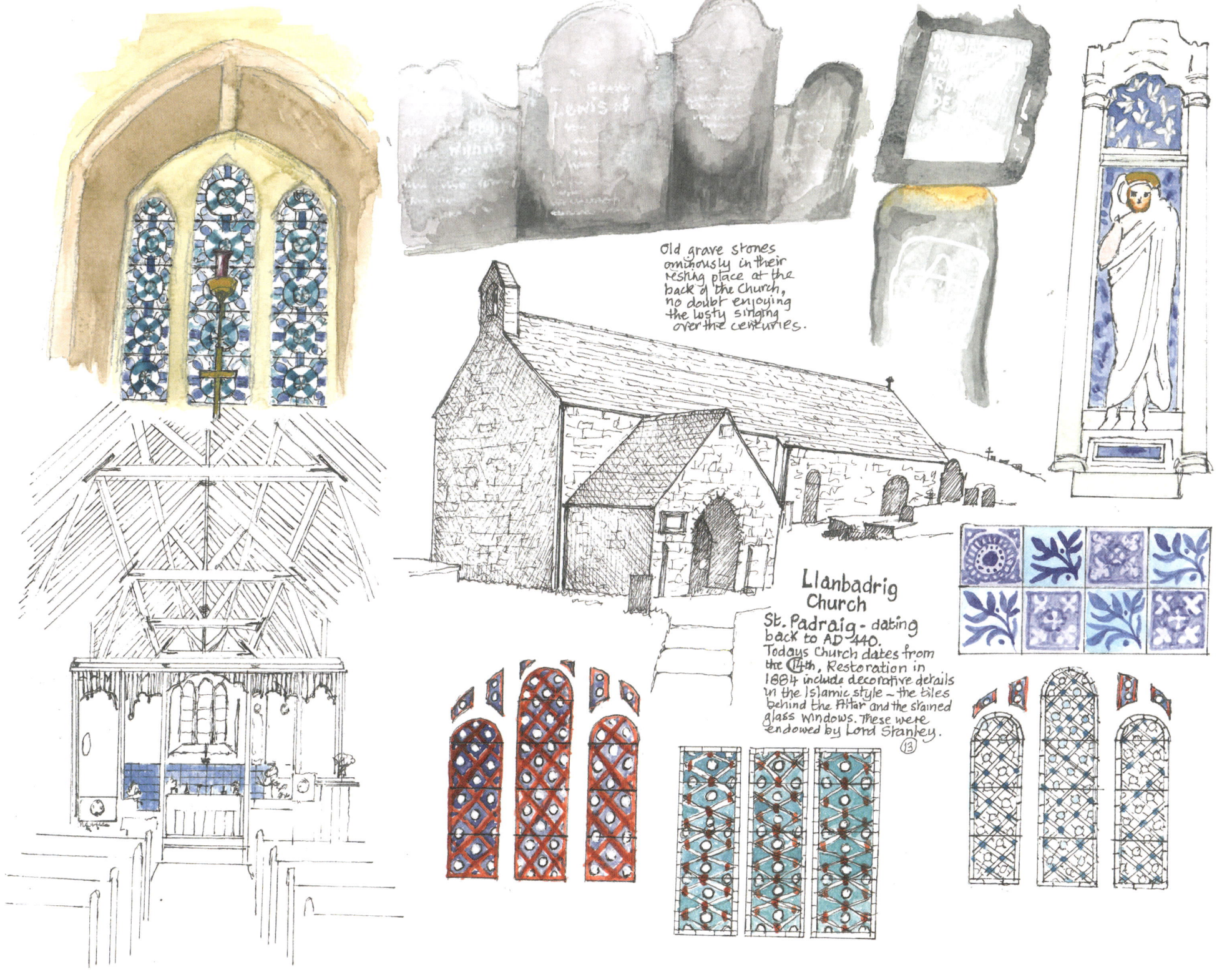

Old grave stones
ominously in their
resting place at the
back of the church,
no doubt enjoying
the lusty singing
over the centuries.

Llanbadrig Church

St. Padraig - dating
back to AD 440.
Todays Church dates from
the C14th, Restoration in
1884 include decorative details
in the Islamic style - the tiles
behind the Altar and the stained
glass windows. These were
endowed by Lord Stanley.

⑬

Conde's a Welsh Liqueurs in their stylishly
elegant bottles.
Made at Bryn Maelin, Llansaeth LL65 4NW
and to be seen and purchased at most
touristy venues. (17)

Bull Bay Hotel &
pretty cottages overlooking
the Bay and Harbour wall at
Bull Bay, Amlwch (38)

72 swans counted
in early November
— out on the water of
the Inland Sea
— amazing! (50)

"Four Mile Bridge"
connecting Anglesey to Holy Island.
The 'Inland water' fills up with the rushing tide
and at low tide empties again with amazing gushing
through the narrow outlet. The power of the water
going either in or out is a constant draw to watch if
you walk the narrow footpath by the road.

'Open as usual' — once when
it snowed prior to Christmas
Y Gegin Fach - Four Mile Bridge (30)

A White Egret seen almost daily on a walk around the Inland Water

The front & the back of ancient Welsh thatched cottages at Church Bay. (16)

Shells, sea washed glass and shards softened by time and the turbulence of the tide.

Collect a bucket full to take home and pop on your kitchen window sill. What fun.

Arch & gate of the Church at Church Bay. (16)

The Church of St. Rhuddlad – a daughter of the King of Leinster (Ireland) – consecrated in 570 A.D. The present Church was built in 1858. (16)

The "Lobster Pot" at Church Bay has quite a reputation for Restaurant 'devotees'. (16)

The Jam Factory — off the beaten track.
Follow the signs from the main Rd. between
Llanfaethlu and Cemaes Bay.
We were quite overwhelmed by the huge collection
of metal Advertising plaques — from a time when
Advertising did not rely on T.V. or other media.
There is a Café & a huge selection of Jams, Honey &
other preserves to purchase.

LIPTONS TEA

CAPSTAN MEDIUM CIGARETTES

TEXACO MOTOR OIL

STOCK RENAULT

SCHOOL 15 M.P.H.

SIGNALS AHEAD

DEWAR'S PERTH WHISKY

CASTROL AFTERCARE SERVICE

Mobilgas

BP

nu-TEXA Brake and Clutch Linings STOCKIST

ESSO

HOSPITAL

SCHOOL SLOW

ASK FOR DOMINION Guaranteed. 1'5

MOTOR "BP" SPIRIT

COLMAN'S STARCH

1'4½

CHURCHMAN'S No 1 Virginia Cigarettes TOBACCO

HOTEL

Mobiloil

Esso

AUTO CLUB OF VIRGINIA AAA EMERGENCY SERVICE

CLEVELAND

ROAD JUNCTION

Morello Cherry with Kirsch made in Anglesey

DRINK VIMTO SOLD HERE

BLUE BELL TOBACCO

MOTORI

HUMP BRIDGE

Brooke Bond Tea

BRASSO METAL Polish

ST JULIEN TOBACCO CIGARETTES

DUNLOP

RAC Rescue Service

CROSSING GATES

REDGATE SOLD HERE Table Waters

Llynnon Windmill

Reconstruction after a storm in 1984

"Melin Hermon"
Another stour handsome reminder of times gone by. This old windmill now sits in someone's back garden in the village of Hermon – perhaps waiting for the day that someone should convert it into another interesting dwelling or a holiday "let."

Why do we all love windmills? And this one is spectacular. On first sight you have to say – WOW! It is placed higher up than the carpark, so on first arrival it is viewed from below which makes it even more impressive.
We had a delicious lunch here as there is a 'home made' café on site, and also two selling areas. It is the oldest working mill in Wales and visitors are able to watch the workings. It is open between Easter and October.
The mill is signed from the village of Llanfacnraeth.
There used to be 50 windmills in Ynys Môn. There are many still in evidence, some dilapidated others converted.
This mill was built around 1775 at the cost of £550

(41)

HOLYHEAD MARINA

Sunday morning in early September at the Holyhead Marina. The Holyhead lifeboat just returning to tie up. Boats of every type and size jostle side by side but many exude a certain glamorous[20] life style ~ a very expensive hobby.

Lifeboats

17-41

My Way Sea **Fishing Trips**
Holyhead Marina
Tel 01248 716315
Mbl 07971 924046
www.goangling.co.uk

TURBINE TRANSFERS
Offshore Wind Farm Workboats
www.turbinetransfers.co.uk

ADVENTURE SAILING SCHOOL.CO.UK

MARAI

Holyhead Breakwater
~ 1.5 miles long
— seemingly into infinity.
It was designed and constructed
between 1845 – 1873, culminating
in a lighthouse designed by John
Hawkshaw.
The huge limestone facing blocks
came from quarries at Moelfre, but
the infill was rock from Holyhead
mountain.
The new Harbour could shelter 100 or
more ships in a storm.
It must have been quite marvellous
to see this feat of construction underway
(20)

The
Wall bends
to the right at
the end.

A "stride out", NOT
for the faint hearted.
Simple design but
an immense & awe-
some undertaking
for the 1850's workmen.
(20)

It is worth a visit to this almost 2 mile stretch of Breakwater.
It is certainly easier to walk along it if the weather is tranquil
but can be exhilarating if the sea is at all choppy.
The Sea is a mighty force and its difficult to imagine all the
labourers between 1845 – 73 building further and further
out into the Sea, so that a Harbour could be protected.
When the last stone went in, what excultation must have
ensued, BUT, at the end of a job, where to go next?
The main growth of Holyhead happened during this time when
workers came from all over the British Isles to work on the wall.
The population of nearly 4000 swelled to almost 9000 as Port
facilities, a new Dock, Station + Hotel were all completed around 1880.
The Port began handling containers as early as 1920 and obviously
continues to this day.
During the depression ('30s) when 1/3rd of the Holyhead workforce was
unemployed, men and boys enlisted in the Southern Whaling & Sealing
Co. Throughout the second World War (39-45) the Port was a Naval Base.

The Breakwater seen from Holyhead Mountain — An awesome feat.
(20)

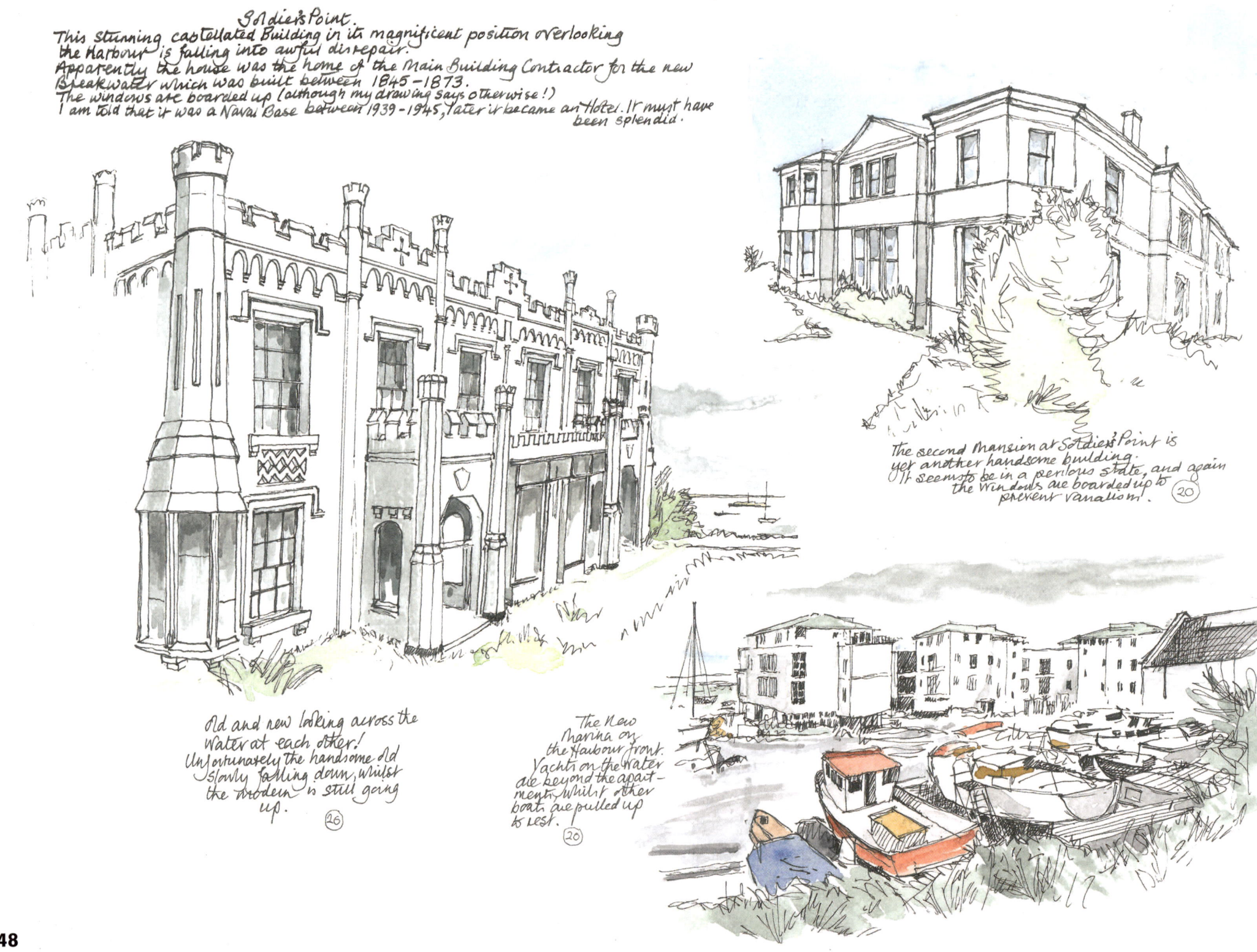

Soldier's Point.

This stunning castellated Building in its magnificent position overlooking
the Harbour is falling into awful disrepair.
Apparently the house was the home of the Main Building Contractor for the new
Breakwater which was built between 1845-1873.
The windows are boarded up (although my drawing says otherwise!)
I am told that it was a Naval Base between 1939-1945, later it became an Hotel. It must have
been splendid.

The second Mansion at Soldier's Point is
yet another handsome building.
It seems to be in a perilous state, and again
the windows are boarded up to
prevent vandalism. 20

Old and new looking across the
water at each other!
Unfortunately the handsome old
slowly falling down, whilst
the modern is still going
up. 26

The New
Marina on
the Harbour front.
Yachts on the water
are beyond the apart-
ments, whilst other
boats are pulled up
to rest. 20

48

Life in Holyhead.

Vehicles which pour 'in' and 'out' of the ferries daily — connecting Ireland, so that
they are able to receive the GOODS that we all require.
I find it quite exciting, but what a heavy toll on the roads through
Anglesey and Wales. Many are foreign, so must also cross England to return
to Europe. (20)

Another very interesting
Building — boarded up,
and very much the worse
for wear.
By the edge of the road
leading into the Car
Park belonging
to Lidl Store in
Holyhead.
(20)

A cheerfully
shamrock
painted Pub.
on Market Street
in Holyhead
'Gleesons'.
(20)

49

'Ucheldre', lurking behind this handsome house in Holyhead. [20]

Sculpture in the garden outside the Ucheldre. Made by Trefor Fôn Owen. [20]

Old windows at Ucheldre [20]

'The Ucheldre' on the skyline overlooking Holyhead. — originally the Chapel of a Roman Catholic convent run by an order of French nuns — closing in 1982 [20]

A lively Art Centre with progressive Art and Sculpture shows, a literary society, dance, multi-media events and film.

There is also a shop and a licensed Restaurant.

Allotment at the side of the Promenade at Holyhead.
It's a romantic notion to think that the allotmenteers are old Seamen who still have the Sea in their sight and in their nostrils as they tend their Gardens. (20)

Behind the allotment — Trusty old Boat friends — pulled up on to the grass. Someones pride and joy! (20)

Grand old metal 'hulk' overlooking the Harbour across from the Marina and 'Cocking a Snook' at posh Yachts across the water. (20)
Sadly in 2015 the Boat has disappeared — to the boat graveyard I fear!

Tower at Soldier Point.
Not serious defence but a 'Folly'.
It is set in the interesting Walls surrounding the castellated Mansion.
(20)

51

HOLYHEAD
Holy Island
Anglesey

St. Cybi's Church
Sitting behind the main shopping
street in Holyhead with a fine vantage
point overlooking the harbour,
and sitting behind the Roman
Fortress walls.
Following the Roman withdrawal
a Christian settlement was founded
here in the 6th by St. Cybi.
The settlement was endowed by
King Maelgwn Gwynedd (died 547)
There were many raids from
Irish Vikings on this Ecclesiastical
site.
The church has many Architectural
styles. The 14th chapel 'Eglwys Bedd'
The present structure dates
mainly from the 15th. The sturdy
tower is 17th and the gilded
fish weather vane was first
placed there in 1793.
The church was restored
between 1877 and 1879.
The Stanley Chapel was built
in 1896-97 and included
lovely stained glass windows
designed by Edward Burne-
Jones and made in the William
Morris workshops.
I am quite intrigued to read that
in the Victorian period there were
14 places of worship, 58 public *
houses and 50 shops in Holyhead.
Holyhead must have been a bustling
community.
* From the Story of a Port
by D. Lloyd Hughes
and Dorothy M. Williams
1981

20

This gravestone is
situated in the grassed
over space in front of
Holyhead Church.
A split gravestone
with a wonderful
testament to one
Patrick Magee (is he
of Irish descent?).
He certainly gained
much respect from those
who buried him
The story is quite moving.

lie the remains of Patrick Magee
who died on the 18th day of November
1849 Aged 79 years
and who during an uninterrupted
arduous Service afloat of 58 years
on the Holyhead Packet Station in
the capacity of Petty officer entitled
himself by his diligence zeal and activity
as such and by his general conduct
to the regard and esteem of those with
whom he served and to the approbation
of the Department of Government
underwhich he served
Also Catherine his wife who died on
the 21st day of February 1836
Aged 65 years
but also included

52

The Millennium Bridge
Holyhead.

A modern alternative to the Menai Strait bridges. It is best seen to its advantage if it is walked upon. It is very sculptural and resembles some sort of writhing stainless steel beast. The bridge connects the station and the port to the town for foot passengers. The stainless steel arches beautifully and although completely different to the suspension bridge must still have proved construction problems. Walk upon it to understand its complexities.

These 'AIRY' boats, sail in the sky at the end of the walk way entering the Holyhead shopping precinct. From the actual walk way they look stunning. "sculpture in the air". Sadly the main street in Holyhead does not have a wonderful selection of shops to browse in. The major superstores are outside the town on the Industrial Estate. However shops like Boots & the major Banks are on the high street. Market day mondays.

looking townwards

Looking towards the Station and Port.

⑳

Looking from the Station back to the Town.
It is interesting to see the scale of the figure in comparison to the width of the steel tubing.

BARGAINS GALORE CASH & C

The very handsome Holyhead Magistrates Court. ⑳

53

Gulls forever sailing above in the sky.
—And children year after year digging their sand castles on the beaches. Ever intent on the work at hand and deriving wonderful enjoyment from their
    buckets and spades and the constructions and moats connected to the sea, and laughing with glee when the sea washes all away—
—another lovely day spent on the beach.

The very attractive Maritime Museum with its scalloped frontage is positioned below Beach Road and overlooking Newry Beach.
    The lovely building is 200 years old, so must have experienced many happenings in every sort of weather over the long period.
    The Harbour Front Restaurant/Bistro is conveniently placed alongside the museum, for visitors who might like to have a meal or a snack.
    The museum is open from Easter to the end of October — DAILY

Another Thomas Telford Tollhouse.
This one is often used as a tea room.

who can say what this prisoner like tower was built for.?

The Pets Cemetery

PIP

REX

BRUNO

MICK

PERRY

-TINY-
(POODLE)
SEPT 1971 - SEPT 1987
16 YEARS A FRIEND
AND COMPANION

says it all!

An entry to a secret garden? In Winter with snowdrops pushing through the earth.

Penrhos

I imagine that this "folly" of a small ruined castle was built either as a shelter from the rain, a picnic venue or as a fort lookout for children. Whatever its purpose, it has a happy feel to it!

This old sundial or bird bath is at the cross-roads of garden paths. In my head I see the Victorian Lords and Ladies sweeping down the paths in their cumbersome frocks enjoying the delights of their garden. My friend now sits here to rest with her dog!

TUNNICLIFFE'S SEAT

Tunnicliffe's seat

The MODERN Anglesey and the very mysterious ANCIENT Stones which Soar into the sky also.
28

Penrhos-feilw
- 10 feet high
- from the second Millennium B.C.
A pair of standing stones.
27

R.A.F. Valley
where young men soar into the sky to be proficient in their Aeroplanes.

permanently grounded outside the Airfield

Llanfaethlu
- mysterious standing stone 10 ft. high - dated 4000 years ago.
Ancient timeless sculptural shapes pointing skywards. They have a simple presence which is quite moving.
17

Llandegfan Stone 51

Presaddfed Burial Chambers.
26

Llanfechell Triangle about 2 m. high

13

Hut circles on Holyhead mountain known as
Ty Mawr hut group ~ 8 ancient farmsteads in all.
The settlement goes back 2500 years which
seems very difficult to comprehend. (21)

The ancient with
the 'newish' looming
over it.
Surprising or what?
(21)

"South Stack"
lighthouse ~ a stern
warning to ships in bad weather.
The view is from the path, not from the air.
The ever-present sea continually bashes against these
dangerous rocks. (21)

57

'Ellins Tower'
Once a Summer
house erected in
1868 by William
Owen Stanley for his wife
Ellin. It is now used by
the R.S.P.B. for an
information centre.
Note South Stack
Lighthouse beyond. ㉑

I have been
looking at this
wonderfully 'straight as a die'
wall for 45 years and still wonder
who built it and for what reason. It is on the
Headland between Rhoscolyn and Trearddur
Bay and is an amazing feat for a
drystone wall. ㉒

A stone erected in the memory of Tyger,
a ship's dog who reputedly swam to
shore with four sailors – each clinging
to his collar in turn when their boat
was wrecked on the rocks above
Rhoscolyn headland.
The dog sadly died & did not survive
the ordeal but the stone allows us
all to remember the brave, clever dog ㉓

TYGER
Sep 17th
1819

Saint
Gwenfaens' ancient
well on the headland between
Rhoscolyn and Trearddur Bay
and just before the long wall.
Now who constructed this interesting
well – too many years ago to consider.

skull found on
the shore at
Renrhyn Fadog. ㉔

Trearddur Bay –
A popular Seaside Resort
– the height of the
Summer and a hot sunny
day with visitors
enjoying themselves.

(22)

Trearddur Bay

August Bank Holiday! The best place to be in the sun, waiting for an icecream to cool oneself. (22)

And fetching a hot `cuppa` to the Beach for hubby and self.

No calls today on a lovely day in the sun ~ at Trearddur Lifeboat Station (22)

Enjoying the fresh air and a good book. (22)

The Anchorage Hotel ~ Four Mile Bridge. (22)

Real Dairy Ice Cream 8 Flavours

HUFEN IA YNYS MÔN

Lifeboat Gift Shop OPEN

VILLAGE FETE SATURDAY 1 AUG

The "Coastguard"

Ice-cream cornets for grown-ups.

on his own contemplating

Grandad enjoying "CHIPS"

Dads enjoying "offspring"

All in aid of the 'R.N.L.I.'
22

Trearddur Bay ~ August Bank Holiday

61

An early 1911 holiday home sitting bleakly on the rocky headland overlooking Trearddur Bay. Rather ominous! (22) Named Craig-y-Môr

An interesting view of the smart 'Trearddur Bay Hotel', Bar and Restaurant seen from their their covered heated pool situated in the gardens. A visit for everyone is the very popular Oyster Fair weekend which is held annually in October. Lots of goodies to purchase. (12)

A hefty winch cemented into the headland just beyond Trearddur — must have known much service in past times. (22)

An old anchor taking its chances with the elements — alongside old cottages & annual hollyhocks. They pop up each year without the aid of the Gardener. - Four Mile Bridge

What a surprise to see 'Police Court' in the brick plaque up above the Butchers in Valley. A smart Victorian building The meat and vegetables are good! (9)

Two splendid eating places
reconstructed by Mr. & Mrs Timpson.
The White Eagle is below Rhoscolyn
church on the lane down to the Beach
and has splendid views over the Bay
towards the Lleyn Peninsula.
(22)

The Oyster Catcher is on the
outskirts of Rhosneigr and has
a whacky younger atmosphere.
(29)

Keeping out the Ocean at Rhoscolyn - or perhaps hiding from the Ocean?

Victorian Seaside Retreat.

Gothic, folly or just plain frivolous? Built up on the hillside over-looking Rhoscolyn. Who owned the structure when it was first built. Now divided into Holiday lets.

Rocks, rocks and rocks, Rope and trees at Rhoscolyn. (23)

I have been admiring this piece of rope sculpture (sea!) for 40 years or so. It does begin to settle. Where did this hefty rope originate

Two wind blasted Hawthorn trees on a path through the fields down to the beach at Rhoscolyn

"Ty Crainc" Rhoscolyn. lurking behind this pretend monument. WHO built this and when? And with tongue in cheek!

Who built these rocky steps many years ago and how many feet have traversed up and down on such hard rock that they are hardly worn? Plant life always finds its own way to flourish.

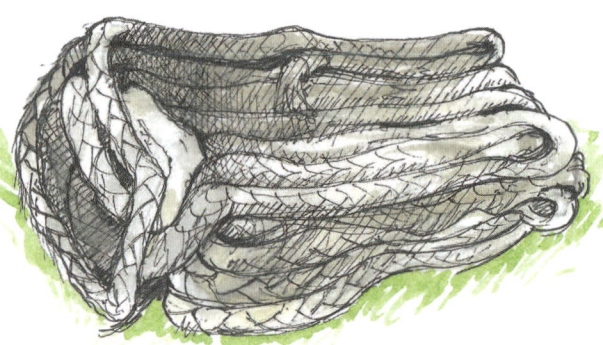

It must have come out of the sea before someone wound it together. How long will it last? — It cannot go on indefinitely as do the ROCKS!

Rhoscolyn Lifeboat Crew.

(drawn from an old photograph)

wonderful characters
from the past (1920s - 30s?)
courageously struggling to
save lives from the sea.

㉓

The audacity of the Chapelgoers to use their vibrant red. The Chapel is planned to be used as a Gallery and Tearoom in the near future. Huge dream for someone.

Church of St. Gwenfaen
Rhoscolyn.

Perched up high on the hillside up above Rhoscolyn Bay and to be seen from all around the surrounding area and from the Sea.

The interior is sweet and simple but does boast to have stained glass by Edward Burne-Jones.

The community hall just a couple of hundred yards away is well used throughout the year, welcoming locals, visitors and even the odd Wedding Party.

The ANGEL in the churchyard appears to watch over all.

(23.)

Two jewel like windows open for all to enjoy in the open porch of St. Gwenfaens Church.

Entrance to
'Cleifiog Uchaf'

Rear of
'Cleifiog Uchaf'

"Cleifiog Uchaf"
The country house Hotel is on
the outskirts of Valley.
Dating from the 16th the House
is steeped in History. Not least,
it being the home of Thomas
Telford whilst he was working
on the Embankment between
Anglesey and the smaller Holy
Island. ⑲

RHOSNEIGR - A busy venue with 3 miles of good sands and dunes - where the Sea rolls in to the shore. A great place for sailing, riding and beach sports.

29.

Domesticity in another converted Windmill quite near to Rhosneigr (Bryn Du).

The same windmill "Felin Isaf" as it used to be.
- probably in Victorian times and next to a largish water source.

As a child we visited Rhosneigr on holiday (horse riding which I did not like!) lasting memories are of this building which my father told us was "Palethorpes Castle". It doesn't look any different today. It is quite "standoffish", but I notice that new modern homes are creeping up to its substantial rear.

65 years ago we visited a Picture Palace to watch 'Red Shoes'. Sadly the venue no longer exists.

A touch of the continental for hungry young things but where is the Bara brith?

Baguettes Croissants Crêpes

MOJOS
F.R.S

A very simple Chapel in Rhosneigr - minus pretentions. On the main street. Definitely grey Welsh.

A nice new little building - The Village Hall, with a jolly Boating weather vane. An interesting change of Architecture in the main street.

Crew of the Rhosneigir Lifeboat in 1883 (from an old photograph) and the SPELLING!

RHOSNEIGR as now.

Lots of stories to be told from the dangerous sea over a hundred years ago.
I wonder about the relevance of the two girls.

CORNER HOUSE
SHOP
PROVISIONS
DRINKS
SWEETS
ICES
ÁBERFFRAW

A neat little blue sign. Unfortunately the window is now bricked up so we guess that trading has ceased.

Another little home in a very dilapidated state. Up a back lane in Aberffraw.

Ripe for a Kyffin Williams sketch or painting

St Buenos church in Aberffraw. situated at the far end of the village. over looking the Sea and the dunes. It's interesting to see the twin roof points.

Hen Bont - Aberffraw
Built in 1731 by Sir Arthur Owen of Bodowen. This old Bridge was not by-passed by the new road until 1932. climb over the bridge to feel a sense of time lessness.

Public house and chapel over-looking each other. Is it with a beady eye?

70

Llangadwaladr ㊶
The Church of St. Cadwaladr

Entry to the
Churchyard.

How long ago, and why
was this beautiful little
window space filled in? ㊶
On this beautiful Spring day,
the stone really did appear
pink & pale green.

The Porch, as entry to this beautiful Church.
It is built from Sandstone; is a Grade 1 listed Building, and has the reputation
of being an Architectural Gem. Certainly on an idyllic early Spring day, our
impressions were of the most exceptionally lovely place — the birds sang in the
trees, the new lambs gambolled beyond the Church railings, & the Churchyard
was awash with snowdrops. As we turned each corner, another lovely
feature met our eye.
The Church is tucked away, — off the main A4080 road, down a small
lane — & what a surprise — history in the making — of now or a 1000 years ago
— and even longer when you read the History Books. Well worth a special
visit.

To go inside would be to absorb more of the Building's special Features!
The atmosphere must be quite something! ㊶
Somebody no doubt will let you in as they must
be exceptionally proud of their heritage.

71

A strange creature lurking by the water pipe (41)

Tucked under the eaves! Who or what is the meaning here? (41)

The handsome Bell tower with Cockerel weather-vane sitting atop. (41)

A Majestic Cross in the churchyard ~ monument to a famous & influential forbear. (41)

And yet another strange creature above a Buttress. No angels here! (41)

And pristine railings surrounding the whole.

Evidence of 100's of years of loving care are to be seen when you take in the delights of this spendid ~ and nearly hidden treasure. (41)

72

windows
of St. Cadwaladr
seen only from the
outside. 41

73

Ynys Llanddwyn
lover's island. (49)

Stepping Stones at
Afon Braint
when were these
impressive blocks wedged
into the river bed?
not for the faint hearted!
(50)

The ruins of Saint Dwynwen's Church
16th century.

Pilot cottages (1826-45) - home to the pilots who guided ships into Caernafon harbour.
Today there is an interesting Exhibition and one house is furnished as it would
have been 100 years ago. A bleak life in winter with their backs to the
prevailing wind and on such an isolated spot.
(49)

The rocky track to
the church of St. Cwyfan
built on its island out in the
Sea. (42)

A mysterious Church interior seen through the window above the Altar
at the Church of St. Cwyfan.
The Church was built in the 1100's, extended in the C14th, a north aisle added
in the C16th but removed in 1800. The Church was restored in 1893, when
a wall was built around the cemetery to prevent erosion. (42)

Steep stone steps
leading up to the
island.
Beware the slippy
lichen which clings
in places to the stairs.
(42)

Saint Cwyfan

75

Anglesey Sea Zoo.

Anglesey Sea Zoo is in a lovely posit-
-ion on the edge of the Menai Strait,
opposite Caernarfon.
  There are lots of interesting watery
Exhibits, a large well stocked shop
where something relevant can be
purchased ~ and a tea room.
  A good educational opportunity
for children - and adults alike.

A birthday to remember ?
For a birthday party
with a difference- try
the Anglesey Sea-Zoo!
We provide everything
from balloons to a huge
chocolate cake! All we
need from you is a motley
collection of young pirates
and little mermaids.

An outing
advertised for
the children !

Fish burrowed
into the sand
with perfect
camouflage;
underwater flowering
creatures and fish
floating by in dark
depths !

House sitting on the Beach side looking out over Menai Strait towards Caernarvon. On the bend going towards the Sea Zoo and the "Anglesey Sea Salt" Industrial Units. ⑤²

Anglesey Model Village & gardens - Newborough LL61 6 RS.

Behind the cottage a surprise of a slate fence - to keep out the animals or divide the garden.

HALEN MÔN

"Anglesey" Sea Salt in its handsome ceramic container with spoon.

Pebbles picked up on the Beach after being tumbled in the sea for unbelievable years ~ 1000's, 10,000, 1,000,000 who can say. But to hold in your palm is to fill you with awe.

charming 'cherry' wallpaper in a ladies bathroom at 'Plas Newydd'.

'Front elevation'.

Plas Newydd

"Plas Newydd" is the family seat of the Marquess of Anglesey, but owing to ill health she is no longer able to live in her private Apartment there. The remainder of the House, its extensive gardens, café and shop are administered by the National Trust.
It was built from Limestone Ashlar stone in the 18th by James Wyatt. It is beautifully positioned on high banks overlooking the Menai Strait across to Snowdonia and during its 'heyday' must have been the most wonderful place to either live in or visit.
Rex Whistler the famous Artist was a friend of the family and the Dining Room is graced with a 58 foot long maritime mural painted by him. There is also an extensive collection of his other work.
Besides the Shop and Café at the entrance, there is also a second hand Bookshop & Coffee shop in the House.

Entry from the Back of the House to a Christmas Craft Fair was a delight to go through banks of Scarlet Horizontale series.
46

78

"St. Mary's Church in the hollow of white Hazel near a rapid whirlpool and the Church of St. Tysilio near the red cave" - Wow, what a mouthful!
This elongated name which is on the old Station is a 19th century 'hoax' - but who's humorous wit decided on this long joke? And how many many innocents have visited, ogled and 'snapped' this Welsh longest name plate?
The Station is a pleasant building, and across a large carpark a vast PRINGLE shop entices shoppers and lots of busloads of visitors
How I enjoyed this challenge with my pen!

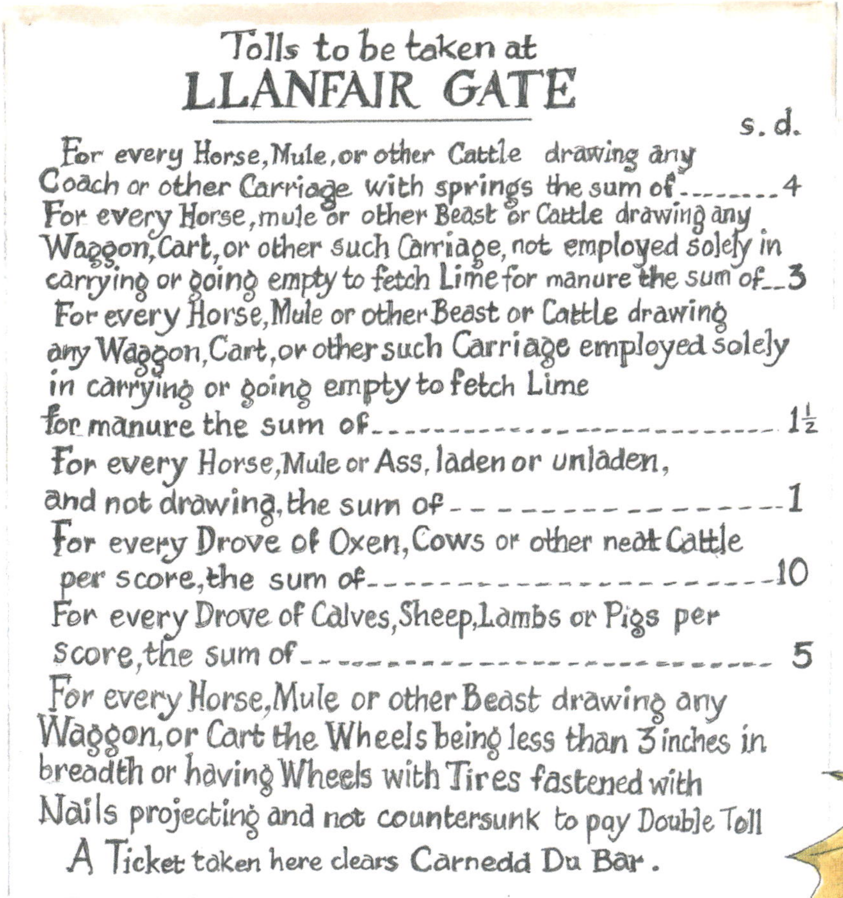

Tolls to be taken at
LLANFAIR GATE

s. d.

For every Horse, Mule, or other Cattle drawing any
Coach or other Carriage with springs the sum of 4
For every Horse, mule or other Beast or Cattle drawing any
Waggon, Cart, or other such Carriage, not employed solely in
carrying or going empty to fetch Lime for manure the sum of .. 3
For every Horse, Mule or other Beast or Cattle drawing
any Waggon, Cart, or other such Carriage employed solely
in carrying or going empty to fetch Lime
for manure the sum of 1½
For every Horse, Mule or Ass, laden or unladen,
and not drawing, the sum of 1
For every Drove of Oxen, Cows or other neat Cattle
per score, the sum of 10
For every Drove of Calves, Sheep, Lambs or Pigs per
score, the sum of 5
For every Horse, Mule or other Beast drawing any
Waggon, or Cart the Wheels being less than 3 inches in
breadth or having Wheels with Tires fastened with
Nails projecting and not countersunk to pay Double Toll
A Ticket taken here clears Carnedd Du Bar.

Lovely crisp leaves littered the floor the day we visited!

A plaque of charges on the old Llanfairpwllgwngyll.
Tollhouse Wall, displaying the charges of the toll in 1895.
Thomas Telford designed five octagonal toll houses which
are across Anglesey on the A5 road.
The tolls are situated at Llanfairpwll, Nant Gate,
Gwalchmai, Caergeiliog and at the entrance to Penrhos
Estate at the end of the Stanley Embankment near to
Holyhead.
(46)

The Marquis of
Anglesey's Column (112ft high)
Seen from the path through the trees at the Car Park.
The Marquis has a wonderful vantage point looking straight
down the Menai Strait towards Caernarfon and down the Welsh
coast. He lost a leg at the Battle of Waterloo and is remembered for
saying when a canon ball hit him - "By God Sir, I've lost my leg" - to
which Wellington replied "By God Sir, so you have". The column is
on the outskirts of Llanfairpwll and is to be seen from many places.

Tacla Taid Transport Museum
on the B4419 between Llangasso
and Newborough. (50)

Three little 'stars' lined up at the museum.

Anglesey Circuit
Tracmôn (29)
Ty Croes, between Rhosneigr
and Aberffraw   LL63

A speedy experience
for those who dare

Huge empty beaches at
Newborough Warren - looking to
the East and to the West.
Plenty of space to run, play
games & go into the sea. (50)
Big skies and Snowdonia
across the Menai Strait in
the distance.

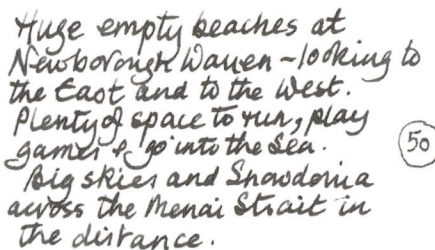

A watercolourist's dream when the
weather is good and if you are more
capable than I !!

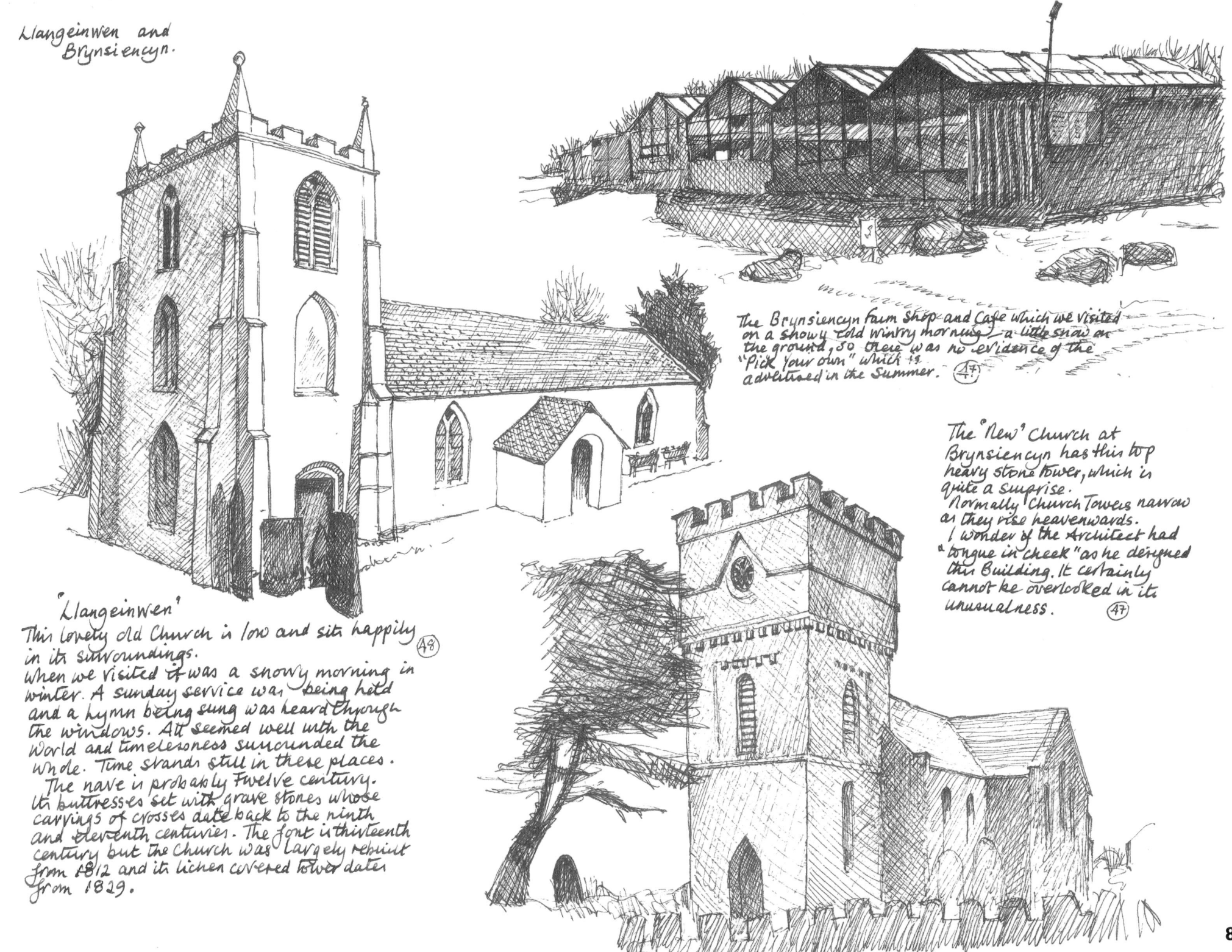

Llangeinwen and Brynsiencyn.

The Brynsiencyn Farm Shop and Cafe which we visited on a snowy cold wintry morning — a little snow on the ground, so there was no evidence of the "Pick your own" which is advertised in the Summer. ㊼

The "New" Church at Brynsiencyn has this top heavy stone tower, which is quite a surprise.
Normally Church Towers narrow as they rise heavenwards.
I wonder if the Architect had "tongue in cheek" as he designed this Building. It certainly cannot be overlooked in its unusualness. ㊼

"Llangeinwen"
This lovely old Church is low and sits happily in its surroundings. ㊽
When we visited it was a snowy morning in winter. A Sunday service was being held and a hymn being sung was heard through the windows. All seemed well with the World and timelessness surrounded the whole. Time stands still in these places.
The nave is probably Twelve century. Its buttresses set with grave stones whose carvings of crosses date back to the ninth and eleventh centuries. The font is thirteenth century but the Church was largely rebuilt from 1812 and its lichen covered tower dates from 1829.

The mysterious 'Bryn Celli Ddu' inviting you into its dark hidden chamber under the mound.
What is it all about? and thinking of Ancestors long long ago is daunting. The stones play such an important part of the History all over the Island.
(53)

A Newborough mat maker about 1900, plaiting the marian grass which grows on the sand dunes.
It was a cottage industry which originally made haystack covers for farmers. Then ropes, mats, baskets and fishing nets evolved. I could imagine that these poor women must have endured very sore hands. I guess that they were very poor.

The "Cob" an embankment built in 1790-1812. Reconstructed after being breached in 1796 - Another Thomas Telford construction. Wonderful coastal defence & a good walk for a dog! (4)

Drawn from a photograph - Edwardian Anglesey II - courtesy of John Cowell.

Detail from the font in Newborough's Parish Church.
The font dates from the (12th).
Weaving grass must have occupied hands for ever it seems.

82

Llangefni.
Spring at Oriel Ynys Môn up
above Llangefni. The buildings are
modern and custom built and provide
a good setting for the regular exhibitions
which are held here.
A new Gallery was added & opened
in 200?. It houses a comprehensive
range of work by the Anglesey
Artist Kyffin Williams.
There is a nice Educational
Area where both
Tunnicliffe's work
and the Massey
Sisters flower
studies are on display
The Gallery, shop and
good Café are open all
year around.
A very nice meal can be
had in the stylish Café.
The staff here are very helpful
and knowledgeable in the
Galleries.

'ORIEL MON'

Next to
the Town Hall,
the imposing
"Bull Hotel"
1852

Interesting properties
going up the hill out
of Llangefni towards
Bodffordd. Unfortunately
as in most towns, supermarkets
have taken the trade from lots of
these small shops, so many are vacant

THE RAILWAY

Another
Welsh Chapel.
Capel Moreia. This one is
on the one way system which takes
you around Llangefni and looks
large enough to fill with those Welsh
singing voices.

The Clock Tower was erected
in 1902 as a memorial
to George Pritchard-
Rayner
of Tre-Ysgawen.
He was 29 when he
died serving in
the Boer War in
South Africa.
The town Hall
was completed
in 1884.

MONA AIR PORT LAND and BUILDINGS. (34)

Carboot Sales are held every Sunday morning. They are very well attended, and particularly if the weather is good. Go early if you expect to find the best bargains. Anglesey Show is held in August, where it seems that every piece of space is taken up – and with plenty of parking. It seems that an awful lot of the population of Anglesey attend and there is an extremly happy and carnival atmosphere. Lots & lots to see and enjoy.

And all those well behaved dogs and children – gobbling their way through hog roast teacakes, pancakes, sausage or bacon baps and any other food from a 'takeaway' vehicle.

Busy, busy busy

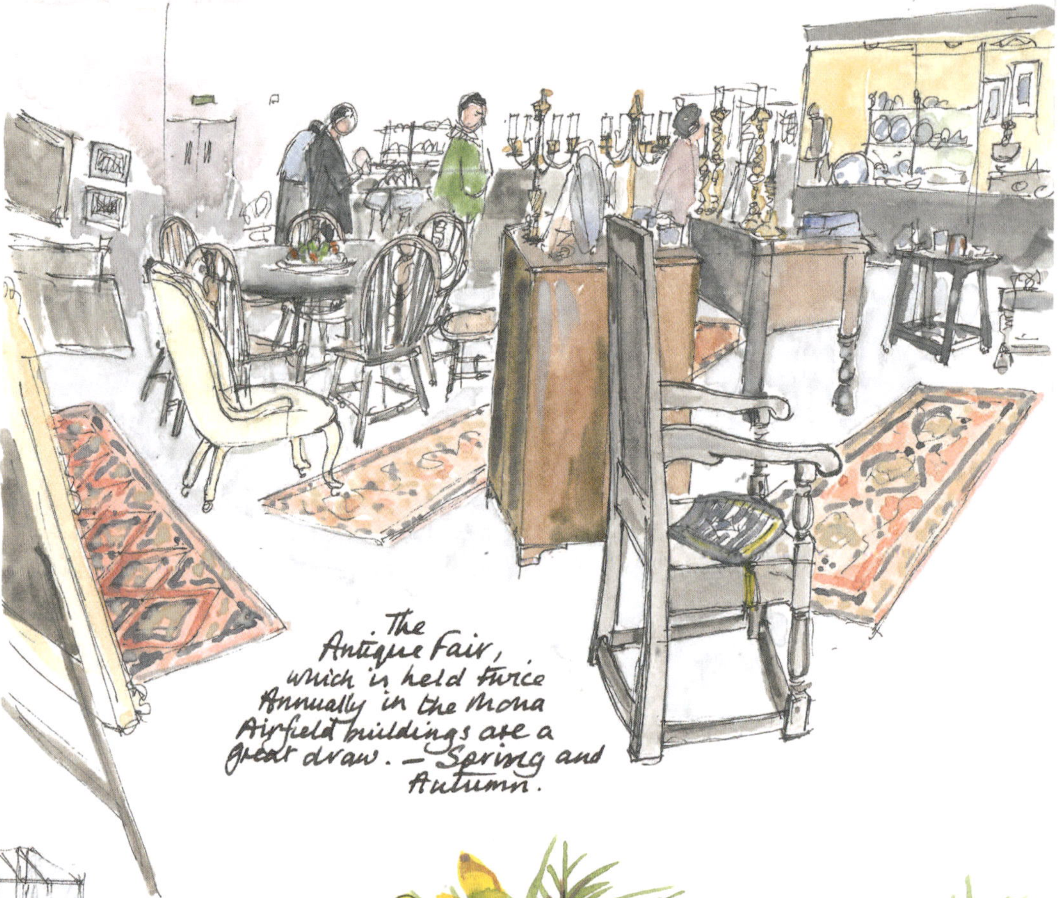

The Antique Fair, which is held twice Annually in the Mona Airfield buildings are a great draw. – Spring and Autumn.

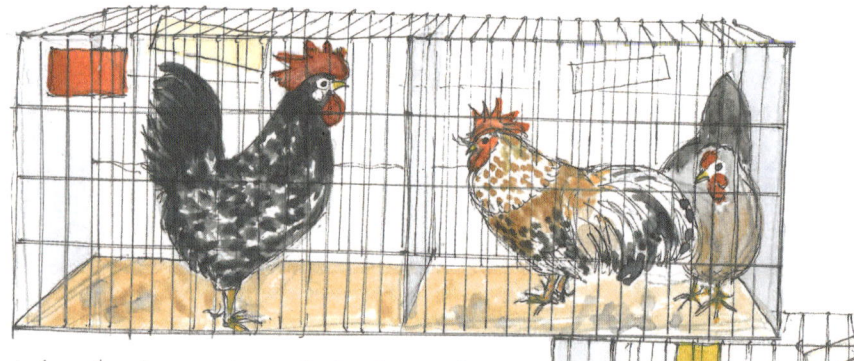

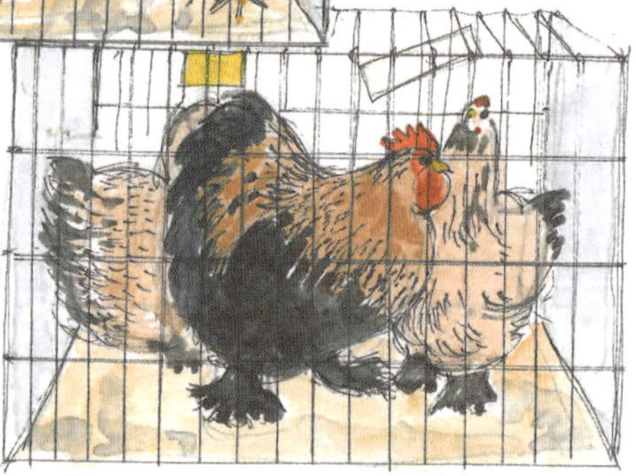

The Anglesey Show is held on this site every Summer for several days, but apart from the Antique Fairs, another 'draw' is the Poultry Breeders Show. What a din going on, and consistent CROWING!

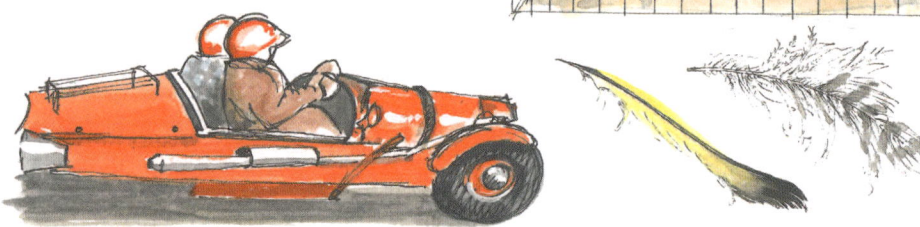

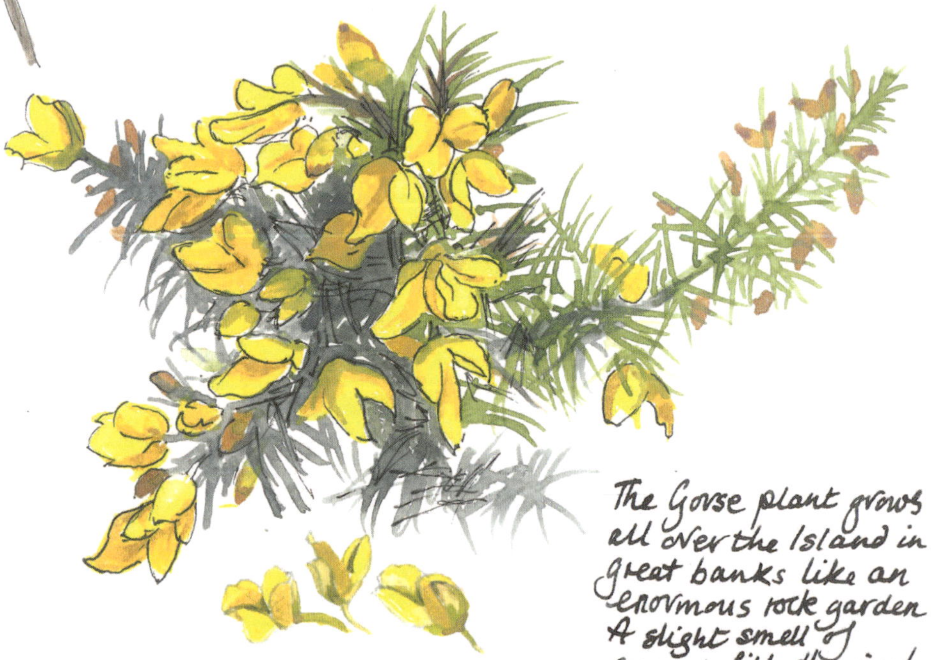

This little car has been known to be seen, zipping around Mona Carboot Sale on a Sunday morning.

The Gorse plant grows all over the Island in great banks like an enormous rock garden. A slight smell of coconut fills the air!

'pigs'

'Horses'

Bonsai trees.

'Anglesey at play'
The Annual Show held on the Mona Showground mid august. 34
—great fun, competitions & just enjoyment.

Whimsical scarecrows to make you laugh!

giant vegetables nearly too good to eat but proudly displayed by the Anglesey gardeners

definitely NOT supermarket onions

lots of modern equipment

hens preening crowing & chortling.

Thomas's having a great day out, but who is this robot-friend?

'Tea-party' cake

well behaved dogs everywhere waiting for a dog show.

posh dahlias

'sheep'

'Rabbit'

'Beet.'

farmers showing their clover grass

grain.

85

The charm of the red
squirrel for which there
is great protection in
Anglesey.
It survives in Newborough
Forest and also at
Penrhos, Holyhead at the
other end of the Island.

The Bulkeley Hotel built in 1837 in the
centre of Beaumaris overlooking the Strait
at the front — at the back over the main
street. The Hotel is built from pleasing
pinky grey large blocks of stone.
   I have an old Book which records the
the travels of a 17 year old girl, coming from London with her sister
and brother on a sketching holiday in North Wales in 1853.
   They travelled from Euston Station to Chester, staying overnight,
then by GIG to Liverpool, & then by boat from Liverpool to the
Bulkeley Hotel. It must have felt very grand being only 16 years
old. It was the month of August, but surprisingly wet and cold.
What can we say to that?
③

A corner in ㊿
the dense
woodland
expanse of
Newborough
Forest.
Do explore for
an invigorating
walk and a
sighting of the
squirrels maybe.

The - Ysgawen Hall was built in 1882, originally
a Country house set in 11 acres of gardens and
woodland. The Hall was originally owned by the
Pritchard - Raynor family, who ran the Copper
Mining Company at Parys Mountain - Amlwch.
   It now boasts to be one of Anglesey's beautiful
homes that is now sympathetically restored.
   Its reputation now is as a fine Hotel and Spa
with heated swimming pool.
   It is a must to eat fine food in the very
gracious surroundings of the dining room.

The - Ysgawen Hall. ㊵

Plas Penmynydd
Llangefni
drawn from an old photograph.
The birthplace of Owen Tudor who married
Queen Catherine, widow of Henry V.
The house is now in
Private ownership.
⑤4

Beaumaris
Gaol
③

An interesting
rear to Plas
Penmynydd

Heraldic devices in the nearby Church
link it to the Tudur or Tudor family of
Penmynydd. They are formed on a finely
carved alabaster tomb of about 1385.
A huge and long standing history swirls in
and out of this fine house.

Picture Perfect Cottage amongst glorious flower beds
at Cadnant Gardens.
Dedication & sheer hard work has paid off, and new
visitors are able to stroll through formal gardens
woodland walks, a study centre and a café.
It was a huge task to undergo, but the result can
only be described as marvellous.
Signed on a road off to the left after you have left
Menai.
②

87

"Bits and Pieces"

Yet another of Thomas Telford's building projects – taking the rail link across Anglesey from the Britannia Bridge to Holyhead and so providing a swift link to Ireland.
Near to Bodorgan: This bridge no doubt is simple in comparison to Anglesey's Suspension Bridges and the Holyhead Millenium Bridge, but how lovely – in its simpleness – and definitely doing the job it was intended for.

Another Toll house at Gwalchmai on the Thomas Telford's A5 road across Anglesey – towards Holyhead.
(34)

Carmel
(31)

Llannerch-y-medd
The Church of St Mary
(37)

Carmel – an 1854 Chapel – just off the road to Llannerch-y-medd. Quite a surprise – the design is so neat and tidy. A small delight! Who attended in its hey day? The jolly red paint on the gate and railings make such a defiant statement. I wonder who decided on the colour – or was it just an odd can of paint left over. – I hope not.

The large stone lychgate is dated 1755, but most of the present church dates from 1840. After storm damage in 1998 the present church opened in 2006.
Llannerch-y-medd was renowned for its fairs and cattlemarkets established in 1657.
At the height of the copperboom 250 cobblers in the town made the footwear for the copper workers. Unbelievable.

WINGS but mainly Seagulls

The Seagull is large, greedy and noisy. It is daring and cheeky and can be quite frightening to little children, BUT it is amazingly clean and invariably looks as if it has stepped out of a Washing machine

Seagull wing found on the shore — so beautiful. Designed by some expert — 12"long. At full flight this bird would be over two feet across. They are generally greedy and seem to gobble anything. They are very loud at times, & there is generally one perched on a high point nearby, but what a joy to see them soaring & sweeping by, so very clean + white.

Another winged creature. An Angel in the graveyard of Rhoscolyn Church. Who made this fine figure with her arm raised heavenwards?
㉓

This wicked seagull (& greedy!) took advantage of a ladies' sandwich at lunchtime — she gave out a large yell, but the seagull had the better of her.

Even keeping an eye on the unsuspecting motorist!

'Copperfields'
Four Mile Bridge

'Copperfields' – Four Mile Bridge. A wonderful small shop selling cotton fabrics, wool and accessories. There's a huge choice; high quality and helpful service by 'devotee' Mary Graves and her pleasant staff. A place of excellence promoting the modern craft of patchworking.

The Welsh ladies stitched their patchwork bedspreads as a way of using up cottons and to keep warm in their beds. If we look at the modern innovative designs that are now being made we are dazzled. No doubt many of the Women's Institute were stitchers, but today many of the designs are shown on Gallery walls. The shop is a dream for anyone who stitches. Quilts are also made in the shop and sold in the Gallery two doors away. Quilts grace many holidaymakers beds.

As you can see there is a rainbow of colours.

30

History being made in Llanfairpwll.

Drawn from an old
photograph — courtesy
of John Cowell
"Edwardian Anglesey II"

The founder members of Llanfairpwll Women's Institute in 1915
    This was the first Institute in Great Britain.
All of the Ladies are hatted and apparently well dressed — and well covered in their best Bombasine for
the occasion. Please note the small dog on the right!
But who are they all? Someones great, great Grandmother perhaps.
They have graciously seated the eldest member to sit in the centre and possibly the chair lady (or
president) is seated second to the right with rotes in her hand and a chain of office around her neck.
I guess that the standing lady on the left owns the garden and she is certainly surveying her visitors.
I should like to have been a 'fly on the wall' at these proceedings — what fun and games + possibly RIVALRY!

General Information :-

Supermarkets on the Island.
Waitrose at Menai Bridge

Asda, Lidl and Aldi at Llangefni

Tesco, Morrisons, Asda, Lidl, Wilco and
Argos at Holyhead.
Other large shopping experiences
eg. B&Q, Currys, Next, TKMax etc
on the Commercial Estate just over the
Bridge and outside BANGOR.

Theres a large garden centre at
Holland Arms and café.
Large 'Pringle' store at Llanfairpwll
which attracts bus loads of customers.
There are Antique Fairs twice yearly
on the Mona Show Ground — in
Spring and Autumn — dates on line.
There is also an Antique & Collectors
Fair held once a month in Beaumaris
     (look on line !)
Tourist Information Centres :-
Amlwch — Industrial Heritage Centre.
Beaumaris — Town Hall, Castle Street
Cemaes — Heritage Centre, High St.,
Holyhead — In the Terminal One of
the Stena-line Port.
Llanfairpwll — Entrance to James
Pringle Weavers shop.

MARKETS
Amlwch — Friday 9am - 4pm
Holyhead — Monday 8am - 4pm
Llangefni — Thursdays and Saturdays
                     8am - 4pm.

"Tongue in cheek". If you are looking for
a screw, a bit of string, welliboots, any
type of paint, coal or bedding plants and
garden pots try STERMAT in Valley.
You can even hire a van or a car.
It is seldom that we come away empty
handed.

Early closing — Post offices & some shops
may close on the afternoons of these days :-
Holyhead and Llangefni ... Tuesday.
Menai Bridge and Beaumaris ...
                          -- wednesday.
Amlwch ... wednesday and saturday.
Benllech ... thursday.

CAR BOOT SALES

Mona Showground - each sunday
                           morning.
Valley --- Tuesday and a quieter
                    one on a thursday
Benllech -- saturdays.

Other Information :-
The wonderfully extensive
"Guide to Anglesey"
  by Philip Steele and
         Robert Williams 2006
has an absolute wealth of
Information.
  It is packed with Historical
facts along with anything else
you might like to find out about
Anglesey and its people.
  It even came up trumps when I
had difficulty finding a Telephone
Number in the Directory.
The Guide includes anything that
you might like to participate in
whilst on holiday —
swimming pools, walking, cycling,
bowls, cricket, fishing, flying,
Golf, horse riding or motor sports.
Rock climbing might be your choice,
Tennis, Watersports, surfing, diving
Kayaks, Sailing.
All are itemised in the "Guide to
Anglesey"
www.llyfrau-magma.co.uk

Acknowledgements :-

Continual encouragement from :-
Pamela Lumsden
Julian and Rodger Kaye.
Invaluable help from :-
Patrick Elwood
Robert Williams (Anglesey Guide)
John Covell — photographs from
               'Edwardian Anglesey'
Brian Thomson MBE
    Coxswain of the Holyhead Lifeboat
Alison Wearne
Jackie Davies   }
Chris Stedham   } Menter Mon
Jane Lewis
Nicola Gibson - Arts officer at Oriel Ynys
                              Môn.

Dafydd Hardy - Estate Agents - Holyhead

Errata:—

Real Bloomers, Page 21 – "The Bull Beaumaris" – Read Charles Dickens, not Shakespeare.
Page 88 – The viaduct carrying the Railway Link to Holyhead was built
by Robert Stevenson, not Thomas Telford.

Since I first did the drawings in my Sketch Book, some of the places have changed. I hope that you can accept that.

And, after completing the Book, I met an inspired young woman who has her own beautiful garden behind the Main Street in Beaumaris (at the Castle end). Go and visit her in the garden and purchase one of her carefully tended plants – or many.